W9-AXH-882

Against Literature

Against Literature

John Beverley

University of Minnesota Press
Minneapolis
London

Chapter 1 originally appeared in *Nuevo Texto Critico* 9/10, 1992;
chapter 4 originally appeared in *Modern Fiction Studies*, vol. 35,
no. 1, 1989; chapter 5 originally appeared in *boundary* 2, vol. 18,
no. 2, Summer 1991; chapter 6 originally appeared in *20th
Century*, vol. 9, 1991–92; chapter 7 originally appeared in *Critical
Quarterly*, vol. 31, no. 1, 1989.

Published by the University of Minnesota Press
2037 University Avenue Southeast, Minneapolis, MN 55455-3092
Printed in the United States of America on acid-free paper

Library of Congress Cataloging-in-Publication Data

Beverley, John.
    Against literature / John Beverley.
        p.   cm.
    Collection of essays, five of which were previously
published, 1989–1992.
    Includes bibliographical references and index.
    Contents: "By Lacan" : from literature to cultural studies—
The formation of the ideology of the literary (from Garcilaso
to Greenblatt)—On the Spanish literary baroque—The
margin at the center : on Testimonio—Second thoughts on
Testimonio—The politics of Latin American
postmodernism—The ideology of postmodern music and left
politics.
    ISBN 0-8166-2248-5 (alk. paper)
    ISBN 0-8166-2249-3 (pbk.)
    1. Criticism—History—20th century.   I. Title.
PN94.B48   1993
801'.95'0904—dc20   92-46356
                                                         CIP

Contents

Preface

The essays collected here represent a critical look from the vantage point of postmodernity at the institution of literature and its ends and means both inside and outside the academy. They are rooted in my work in the field of Spanish and Latin American literature, which is my own version of a local *Gemeinschaft*, but they are intended also as an intervention in the ongoing debates and discussions about what we do in the humanities generally, about close reading, the canon, theory, cultural studies, reception and reader response, multiculturalism, political correctness, values, deconstruction, and the like.

Several readers of the manuscript have noted that these essays as they stand do not quite make a book. I am inclined to agree, but to have modified them further would have taken away their polemical edge. What unifies them, and lends them a meaning together that they did not have in the separate circumstances of their initial publication, is the title, which points to a certain *ressentiment* on my part about my profession and my place in it as the driving force behind them. As a slogan, "against literature" could be read two ways: in the sense of versus, that is, in an antagonistic relation with literature; or, as in a gestalt figure/ground relation, as a performance that has as its necessary condition literature. I would prefer to think that what I am doing is the first of these. But I am aware of the paradox that what my critique stigmatizes as the ideology of the literary remains in some sense inescapable for me. These essays are written within academic humanism (and in one of its most privileged genres), by someone for whom literature has been the main intellectual passion of his life. They are directed to like-minded individuals in and around the academy who, early on in their lives, turned their experience of otherness into a commitment to the field of literature, which was both a consolation and a weapon (and then a possibility of making a living).

To anticipate the inevitable misunderstanding or misrepresentation: by literature I do not mean "literature in general" but the historically specific form it assumes between the fifteenth and eighteenth centuries with the formation of the European vernacular languages, the modern nation-state, colonialism, capitalism and bourgeois culture, movable type technology, the commodification of books and printing, and the modern university and education system. (I do not mean *The Tale of Genji* or the Byzantine novel, in other words.) Although I regard these essays as an extension of the project of what Althusser called a "theoretical antihumanism," I am by no means declaring the "death" or end of literature (the discourse of apocalypse being more appropriate for the right, which has a lot to lose from a change in things), or even proposing that there is any more authentic or effective ground than the one we are on as producers and students of literature. Like Gayatri Spivak, I "don't say that I am *just* a literary critic. I say I *am* a literary critic."[1]

My work as a critic began with a dissertation at the University of California San Diego in the late sixties that was a close reading against the grain of the prevailing interpretations of one of the canonic texts of Spanish Golden Age literature, Góngora's long poem, the *Soledades*, which had been a touchstone of Spanish literary formalism in the Franco era. Fredric Jameson was one of my teachers, and I tried to show, in the fashion of what was to become his idea of a textual "political unconscious," how you could see the pressure, so to speak, of history and ideology inside the *Soledades*, in its very formal mechanisms. My subsequent work on the role of literature in the Spanish colonial Baroque came out of the Góngora study, but also involved something like an inversion of its concerns: I was interested now in registering the pressure of literary texts like the *Soledades on* history and social formations. I wanted to know, to the extent this was possible, how literature "constituted" (in a small but measurable degree) social reality rather than how it "represented" it. I was strongly influenced in this effort by the work of Chantal Mouffe and Ernesto Laclau—itself built on the prior writing of Gramsci and Althusser, and on contemporary poststructuralist and feminist theory—which emphasized in a politically engaged way the discursively constructed nature of society and the human subject itself.

I had been involved since 1978 in solidarity work with Central American revolutionary movements, and this led me to become interested in studying, together with my friend Marc Zimmerman, who was a specialist in this area, the role of literature in their formation. To understand how (for example) Ernesto Cardenal's poetry was influential in the articulation of Sandinist ideology and political mobilization, it was not enough to show what was in the text itself, even in terms of the Jamesonian "positive hermeneutic" I had used in my earlier work on Góngora. We also had to understand how literature functioned as a social-ideological institution with its own special dynamic in Central American society: who read literature, how they read it, what it meant to be involved with literature, the relationship of literature to the state, and so on.

This was not just a question of reception theory or reader-response criticism, however. In their standard forms—phenomenological and empirical, respectively—these approaches also seemed to vitiate thinking about literature as a historically and socially specific institution, among other things because they did not interrogate the historically constructed category of the reading subject itself. It became clear that to produce a theory of the role of literature in the incubation of revolutionary movements in Central America we had to interrogate how literature as an institution was implicated in the colonial formation of Latin America itself and subsequently in the construction and evolution of Latin American nation-states. Literature, we came to see in a way I sketch in part I, not only had a central role in the self-representation of the upper and upper-middle strata of Latin American society; it was one of the social practices by which such strata constituted themselves as dominant. As such, "a change in the notion of literature"—to borrow the title phrase of Carlos Rincón's influential revision of Latin American literary criticism—could imply also the release of previously repressed social energies. Zimmerman and I concluded the book that resulted from our work with the following obser-

vation: "literature has been a means of national-popular
mobilization in the Central American revolutionary process,
but that process also elaborates or points to forms of cultural
democratization that will necessarily question or displace
the role of literature as a hegemonic cultural institution."[2] It
was the recognition of this paradox that set the stage for the
preoccupations these essays involve.

The question of the relation between literature and power
leads me to say something about the other defining force in
them, which is their relation to Marxism and the political
project of socialism. While I understand its concerns, I do
not share the critique of the encapsulation of the left in the
academy voiced most urgently perhaps by Russell Jacoby in
his book *The Last Intellectuals*. I think it ignores the way in
which the university has become a central and crucial institution of contemporary society, particularly in the context of
globalization. Modifying Derrida's famous slogan, I would
risk saying, in fact, that there is no "outside-the-university,"
in the sense that all contemporary practices of hegemony
(including those of groups whose subalternity is constituted
in part by their lack of access to schools and universities)
pass through it or are favorably or adversely affected in
some way by its operations.

The problem of the academic left is a different one: those
of us who, like myself, saw Marxism as the necessary hori-
zon in both ideological and scientific senses of a "Long
March through the institutions," and who were successful
to some extent in bringing new Marxist perspectives into the
Cold War academy, must now confront the paradox of its
collapse or defeat at almost every other level of global society *but* the university. It was never, for most of us who came
from the New Lefts of the sixties, a question of the Soviet
Union or Eastern Europe, although we thought that the obvious problems would be solved by a historically inevitable
process of reform or revolutionary rectification. But the virtual disappearance of "actually existing socialism" in the
Soviet Union and Europe, together with the emergence of
new, untheorized, forms of transnationalization of capital
and communications, place us today in a situation similar to
that of Lenin and Rosa Luxemburg on the eve of the First
World War: that is, facing the need to reinvent, or abandon,

the socialist project as such. There is the inevitable temptation to retire to cultivate our gardens (postmodernism,
cultural studies, writing novels, or gardening plain and
simple).

If the thematics of glasnost and postmodernism have
made both the idea and the reality of third world liberation
struggle somewhat unfashionable today, it is also useful to
recall that for poor Salvadorans—by far the majority of the
population—the living standard and level of general social
decency that were available to, say, Polish or Cuban workers
under socialism are utopian (they have lived for the last decade under a nominally "democratic" regime sustained by
several billion dollars in U.S. aid, which nevertheless has
found it necessary to kill some seventy thousand of them).
What I would modify in these essays today, on the heels of
the uprising in Los Angeles that followed the verdict in the
trial of the police officers who attacked Rodney King, is the
rather uncritical enthusiasm for postmodernism that they
display. In jumping on the postmodernist bandwagon, I was
following the dictates of my taste: I genuinely *liked* and identified with television, pop art, Laclau and Mouffe, DeLillo,
punk rock, Philip Glass and the American minimalist com-
posers, *The Kiss of the Spider Woman*, Gehry's Santa Monica
house, and the like. I also saw postmodernism as a way out
of the crisis of the left that was already in evidence by the
beginning of the eighties, a crisis I experienced personally in
the form of my involvement in the merger of the New American Movement and the Democratic Socialist Organizing
Committee (DSOC) that led to the formation of Democratic
Socialists of America (DSA). In my turn to postmodernism,
there was an element both of what Jameson has called the
"aesthetic populism" of the New Left and of the impatient
petty-bourgeois radicalism of the sort that made the displacement of the enthusiasms of the "brief Golden Age"
(Brecht's phrase in *The Caucasian Chalk Circle*) of May '68 onto
the poststructuralist sublime of Baudrillard, Kristeva, and
company relatively painless.

Unfortunately, history is not a great respecter of the tra-
jectory of individual lives or careers. I still think that the considerations about the relation between postmodernist sensibility and the reconstruction of the left in these essays are

important, in the sense that they allow us to see some of the left's emergent forms. But I am more inclined today to play down the notion that we have entered some kind of qualitatively new stage of things—"New Times." We are clearly in something like a new stage of capitalism. But that is not the same thing as a fundamentally new way of organizing human relations and value, a new mode of production. Modes of production are, like neuroses, a "structure," and structures are (the language may sound somewhat antiquated, recalling those introductions to structuralism we all had to wade through, but it is no less relevant) synchronic. Which means that they do not (outside of their self-representation in ideology) have a history; they go on determining, but not being reciprocally modified by, processes of external growth and change. Only with great patience and difficulty—and then only partially—can they be undone (but they can be undone).

Laclau and Mouffe have noted that in the notion of post-Marxism, which they embrace, the stress can fall either on post or Marxism. In the first case, what is really implied is anti-Marxism: it was all a bad mistake, of the "God that failed" sort, from which one would be well advised to beat a quick and effective retreat. In the second, if someone asked you what sort of person you are ideologically, you could answer "I'm a post-Marxist Marxist" (perhaps in the spirit of the remark attributed to Marx on his deathbed, that he was not a Marxist). If that is the sense post-Marxism conveys, then I have no problem embracing it either, particularly if it also means that the disasters or impasses produced by the various forms of Marxism-Leninism and social democracy are not the last word in that process of struggle for a better world that Marxism itself invoked and sought to be the theoretical form of. In Latin America, at any rate, the "crisis of Marxism" goes at least as far back as Mariátegui's powerful attacks in the twenties on Eurocentric models of history and national development in his *Seven Essays on Peruvian Reality*. Whenever the Latin American left reinvents itself (as it is in the process of doing now), it has risked the charge of having left some kind of Marxism behind. There is no question that any number of Marxisms have become "post" in Latin America, as elsewhere in the contemporary world. But in the face of the intensification of the exploitation of the working classes and popular sectors, the debt crisis, and the integration of Latin America into global postfordism it portends (so that the fifties now come to be seen nostalgically as a kind of lost Golden Age everywhere), it would be premature to claim the same for the Marxist impulse as such, or for the social conditions that it reflects and theorizes.

The animus against literature that these essays carry is due above all to literature's connection with the formation of the modern state and the conditions of maintaining and redefining capitalist hegemony, particularly in situations of colonial or neocolonial domination. But what happens if literature becomes detached, partially or wholly, from this function? This is more than a hypothetical question, given the present disarticulation of the nation-state's own capacity to structure relations and meaning, on the one hand, and the relative democratization and proliferation of literature that modern public education produces, on the other. I have in mind here the way the literature I studied in the book with Marc Zimmerman condensed ideologically popular and middle-sector antagonisms toward the state in Central America, or the way (as Yvonne Yarbro, Mary Louise Pratt, and others have been noticing) Chicana feminist and lesbian writers like Gloria Anzaldúa are using poetry and narrative to redefine and reenergize a previously male-centered identity politics, preparing the ground perhaps for the emergence of new forms of liberation struggle. In Pratt's metaphor, literature used in this way can serve as a kind of "contact zone" where previously disarticulated subject positions, social projects, and energies may come together.[3]

Edward Said's magisterial *Culture and Imperialism* (New York: Alfred Knopf, 1993) appeared as I was correcting the proofs of this book. Its coincidence with my concerns here on any number of points will be evident, particularly in its analysis of the way Western literature in general, and the novel in particular, constructed the imaginary of colonialism and imperialism. But if for Said literature is therefore part of the problem, it is also, in his anticipation of the emergence of a new postcolonial, transnational humanism modeled on the work of writers like Frantz Fanon, Salman Rushdie, Elias Khoury,

Gabriel García Márquez, or Toni Morrison, part of the solution, "another way of telling," in his words. Would that it were so (against the seemingly implacable logic of global capitalism, Said himself writes very much in the mode of Gramsci's injunction, "pessimism of the intellect, optimism of the will"). But the burden of these essays is to question whether literature can or should continue to be the privileged signifier of the desire for a more egalitarian, democratic, and ecologically sound social order that underlies what Immanuel Wallerstein calls "anti-systemic movements" in the contemporary world. It is not only Khomeini-style fundamentalisms (or, for that matter, the realpolitik of the Indian government) that may have problems with the aesthetic and ideological strategies represented by a novel like *The Satanic Verses*. In something that is so obviously connected via the education system to the state and to the formation of elites, there is always the danger that even the most iconoclastic or "progressive" literature is simply forging the new forms of hegemony. On the other hand, I do not think that there is some more privileged or effective space for the constitution of a politics of resistance or counterhegemony than the education system itself, and it is difficult to imagine a human future in which variants of what we know today as literature will not play some role in the definition of new forms of human liberation and possibility. (Any temptation to romanticize the preliterary may be dissipated by recalling that at the time of the American Revolution slaves were legally enjoined from learning how to read or write.)

It is not just a question of literature as such, then, but of *what* counts as literature, and how it is used. In the case of a text like *I, Rigoberta Menchú*, which is a repeated concern in these essays, it is not only the adequacy of the "readings" we can produce, but the ways in which these adjust themselves to the requirements of the struggle for liberation (or simply for survival) that are implicated in its situation of enunciation. Because this is a matter of participation and solidarity, and not of charity or liberal guilt, however, perhaps Rigoberta Menchú's own words are a more helpful instruction: "Cada uno de nosotros tiene que conocer nuestra realidad y optar por los demás"—each of us has to understand our own reality, and then opt for others.

Acknowledgments

The idea for the book, and parts of the Preface and chapter 1, appeared originally as an essay in *Osamayor* II, 3 (1990), the review of the graduate students of the Department of Hispanic Languages and Literature of the University of Pittsburgh. The central section of chapter 1 appeared originally in Spanish as " 'By Lacan': Crisis del marxismo y política cultural en las Américas" in the proceedings of a conference at the University of Sassari in Sardinia on the work of Roberto Fernández Retamar, *Calibán en Sassari*, edited by Hernán Loyola and published as a special issue of *Nuevo Texto Crítico* 9–10 (1992). It is translated here by permission. A somewhat different version of the first part of chapter 2 was intended as a chapter titled "Humanism, Colonialism and the Ideology of the Literary (On Garcilaso's Sonnet 23)" for a forthcoming collection, *New Hispanisms*, edited by Paul Julian Smith and Mark Millington. The second part, on Stephen Greenblatt's *Marvelous Possessions*, was given as a lecture at the 1992 Modern Language Association in San Francisco. Chapter 3 is an expanded version of a piece that appeared as "On the Concept of the Spanish Literary Baroque" in volume 7 of the Hispanic Issues series, *Culture and Control in Counter-Reformation Spain*, edited by Anne Cruz and Mary Perry (Minneapolis: University of Minnesota Press, 1992). Chapters 4, 6, and 7 are slightly edited and revised versions of the original articles: "The Margin at the Center: On *Testimonio*," *Modern Fiction Studies* 35 (Spring 1989) (a special issue edited by Timothy Brennan on *Narratives of Colonial Resistance*); "Postmodernism in Latin America," *Siglo XX/20th Century* 9 (1991–92); and "The Ideology of Postmodern Music and Left Politics," *Critical Quarterly* 31, 1 (1989). They are reprinted here with the permission of their respective publishers. (My thanks to Colin MacCabe in par-

ticular for inviting me to present the piece on music in a lecture series on postmodernism he organized at the University
of Pittsburgh some years ago.) Chapter 5 derives from a
paper I presented at a conference at the Kellogg Institute of
the University of Notre Dame, organized by Steven Bell,
on Narrative Practices and Cultural Discourse in Latin
America, in March 1990. It appeared in *boundary* 2 18, 2
(Summer 1991) under the title " 'Through All Things Modern: Second Thoughts on Testimonio," and is reprinted here
in a considerably shortened version with permission of the
publisher, Duke University Press.

Let me also acknowledge the friends, students, and colleagues who have shared in one way or another the concerns and commitments represented by these essays: Hugo
Achugar, Antonio and Cristina Cornejo-Polar, Marina Cat-
zaras, Aristidis Baltas, Liana Teodoratu, Julio Ramos, Beatriz
González, Lucia Costigan, Billy and Eduardo Lozano, Guil-
lermo Mariaca, Eva Bueno, Michael Aronna, Victorien La-
vou, Michele Soriano, Michele Ortuño, Tony Higgins, Juan
Zevallos, Niraj Pant, José Oviedo, Marc Zimmerman, Dave
Houston, Joe and Delsa White, Ran Mitra, Alice and Adrian
Birney, Cynthia Steele, Paul Smith, George Yúdice, Roberto
Fernández Retamar, Ambrosio Fornet, Paul Bové, Hernán
Vidal, Jules Lobel, Iris Young, Ed Baker, Bridget Aldaraca,
Ileana Rodríguez and the members of the Latin American
Subaltern Studies Group, and Carl Kirschner and his col-
leagues in the Rutgers Spanish Department. Special thanks
to Anita Roy of Manchester University Press and Biodun
Iginla of the University of Minnesota Press for believing in
the possibility of this book, and to Neil Larsen, Jean Franco,
and Fred Jameson for reading and commenting on the
manuscript at various stages. In more ways than one, these
essays are a part of a continuing discussion/debate with
Jameson, whose example as a teacher and critic was decisive
in the formation of their concerns. The other name that occurs frequently in them is that of Gayatri Spivak, who as
both a colleague and a comrade has challenged me over the
years to work against the grain of my own prejudices, allowing me to see and say things I would not have otherwise.
This book is for my daughter Alisa, now five, my wife, Gay,

in celebration of (among many other things) our twenty-fifth wedding anniversary, and my brother, Jim, in anticipation of his fiftieth birthday, and in memory of our mother, Edith Pilcher Beverley (1910–93), who died as I was finishing it: "Todo lo mudará la edad ligera / por no hacer mudanza en su costumbre" (Garcilaso).

CHAPTER 1

"By Lacan": From Literature to Cultural Studies

Gayatri Spivak recounts the following anecdote:

After my public lecture on "Literature and Life" in March 1980 at Riyadh University Center for Girls (*sic*), a student asked me with some asperity: "It's all very well to try to live like a book; but what if no one else is prepared to read? What if you are dismissed as an irresponsible dreamer?" I found an answer to her question at the tail end of a metaphor: "Everyone reads life and the world like a book. Even the so-called 'illiterate.' But especially the 'leaders' of our society, the most 'responsible' non-dreamers: the politicians, the businessmen, the ones who make plans. . . . Yet these leaders read the world in terms of rationality and averages, as if it were a textbook. The world actually writes itself with the many-leveled, unfixable intricacy and openness of a work of literature. If, through our study of literature, we can ourselves learn and teach others to read the world in the 'proper' risky way, and to act upon that lesson, perhaps we literary people would not forever be such helpless victims."[1]

Spivak proposes here a sense of literary textuality as a pedagogic model for nonliterary social and political practices; my intention in these essays is rather to produce a negation of the literary that would allow nonliterary forms of cultural practice to displace its hegemony. Perhaps her project of "unlearning privilege" and my own are ultimately convergent—I suggest as much in my discussion of testimonial narrative in part II. I know that her intention is to empower cultural practices that can go beyond the patriarchal, colonial, and imperialist construction of the world system. But I am hesitant to endorse the self-satisfaction of the

1

literary her statement (and the general appeal of deconstruction to a notion of social "textuality") displays. Is there not in fact a way of thinking about literature that is extraliterary, or as I prefer here, "against" literature?[2]

For we are long past thinking of literature as a universal; rather, we tend to speak today of "literatures" with historically and socially specific conditions of production and reception—"reading formations," to use a concept Tony Bennett has developed.[3] In relation to Latin America, the obvious starting point in this respect is the fact that one of the things—along with Christianity, smallpox, and the *encomienda* system of forced labor—Columbus and his successors brought with them to the New World was the institution of literature, in the form it is given in Europe by the doctrine and teaching of the Humanists, the vernacular literature of Petrarch and the Italian Renaissance, and the technology of movable type, which allowed for the mass production of printed books.

This fact has endowed Latin American literature with an ambiguous cultural role and legacy: literature (or, less anachronistically, *letras*) is a colonial institution, one of the basic institutions of Spanish colonial rule in the Americas; yet it is also one of institutions crucial to the development of an autonomous creole and then "national" (although perhaps not popular-democratic) culture. Whatever their differences, when, for example, Gabriel García Márquez, Mario Vargas Llosa, or Elena Poniatowska write today, there is a sense in which their work and the impact it has on its public still bears the traces of this paradox. As Angel Rama argued, a "republic of letters" (*ciudad letrada*) and the consequent role of the writer as a political-moral leader are among the basic forms of institutional continuity between colonial and contemporary Latin America.[4]

As Rama shows, literature develops in very close relation to the state in Latin America. What is shared by both sides in the ongoing debate about the significance of the Baroque in Latin America, which I look at in chapter 3, is an agreement about the centrality of literature as a social practice among the Spanish and creole elites. The differences have to do with what sort of ideological valence to assign this centrality: colonial and Eurocentric, in the case of the anti-

Baroque position; creole or protonationalist in the case of the pro-Baroque position. For literature to have this kind of centrality involves a socially and historically determined *overvalorization* of its importance and function. Directly or indirectly connected to this fact is the almost unchallenged assumption in Latin American literary history—its origins are in the work of Pedro Henríquez Ureña, the founder of modern Latin American literary criticism—that the writing of the colonial and independence periods was a cultural practice that models the national. This assumption, which makes literature and literary values the key signifiers of regional identity for a national-bourgeois intelligentsia, became institutionalized as part of the ideology of the humanities in the Latin American university system.[5]

In the context of the appearance the Latin American novel of the Boom represented by writers like García Márquez and its conjunctural coincidence with the political effervescence generated by the Cuban Revolution in the sixties, there was, on the part of both authors and critics in Latin America and the Caribbean, a similar idealization of the role of literature as an instrument of national liberation. Its extreme was perhaps Julio Cortázar's identification of the function of the avant-garde writer or artist with the guerrilla *foco*; but Rama himself, in his work before *La ciudad letrada*, championed a form of left literary modernism, arguing that the sort of writing represented by the Boom novelists could be an agency of "narrative transculturation," borrowing the term from the Cuban ethnographer Fernando Ortiz, who used it to describe the creative interaction of European and African elements in the formation of modern Cuban culture. The wide dissemination and popularity of the Boom novels, and the sudden urgency lent to things Latin American by the Cuban Revolution allowed for the expansion of the global audience for Latin American literature and its reprioritization as a field in the European and North American university system, where it had traditionally been overshadowed by Spanish literature.

It would have spoiled the party to point out that this idealization of literature, which seemed so modern and radical, was simply reactivating an element of Latin American colonial and oligarchic culture. But notably absent in the celebration of the "new" Latin American novel of the Boom was much attention to the way in which literature might continue to function as an apparatus of alienation and domination: to the "unconscious," so to speak, of the literary.[6]

The reader will by now have recognized the phrase "By Lacan" in the title of this chapter as an anagram of Caliban, in turn Shakespeare's anagram in *The Tempest* of cannibal, that is, of one of the dominant characterizations by Europeans of the indigenous populations of the New World in the sixteenth century. In his classic essay of the period of armed struggle in Latin America, Roberto Fernández Retamar suggested the figure of "deformed Caliban" as the allegorical representation of Latin American culture.[7] Retamar was responding to the Uruguayan writer Rodó, who almost a century earlier had posited Ariel—the "creature of air," the writer-poet—in this role as the antithesis of the values represented by U.S. culture.

Cannibal/Caliban/By Lacan: the sequence of names configures the stages and the historical subjects of, respectively, the colonization, decolonization, and postcoloniality of Latin America. What is significant, however, is that the anagram works only in English now. It calls to mind Rubén Darío's apocalyptic question in his poem "Los cisnes" about the future of Latin America in the face of the massive onslaught of U.S. imperialism at the turn of the century: "¿Tantos milliones de hombres hablarán inglés?" (so many millions, will they all speak English?), and his invocation, in "A Roosevelt," of the "futuro invasor / de la América ingenua que tiene sangre indígena, / que aun reza a Jesucristo y aun habla en español" (future invader / of the innocent America which has Indian blood, / which still prays to Christ and still speaks in Spanish).

The imposition of English in Latin America was the outcome for Darío of the failure of a properly Hispanic modernity, perhaps the modernity represented by the Liberal regime of José Santos Zelaya in Nicaragua at the turn of the century, a regime that Darío himself supported and served and that was overthrown in the first of many interventions by the U.S. Marines in Nicaragua in 1907. English would, in this context, be the language of a possible vector of Latin

American postmodernity. "Sangre indígena" y "aun reza a Jesucristo," on the other hand, refer back to the pre-Columbian civilizations and to the heritage of Spanish Catholicism; that is, to the persistence within Latin American social formations of a premodernity resistant to liberalism and the full development of capitalist rationality.

Retamar's revision of the figure of Caliban was meant to signify the originality not only of Latin American culture but also of its human agent, represented by masculine writer-heroes like José Martí, Vallejo, Che Guevara, Fanon, or Carlos Fonseca Amador—men of action formed decisively by literature and the humanities. "By Lacan" suggests instead the "desiring subject" revealed in psychoanalytic theory and practice, whose sense of inner lack can never be compensated; the consumer instead of the producer; Molina instead of Valentín in Puig's *Kiss of the Spider Woman*; Walter Benjamin with his hashish and his love of the Arcades instead of the puritanical Adorno; the eighties instead of the sixties; Manuel Puig or Rigoberta Menchú instead of Mario Vargas Llosa or Carlos Fuentes; television instead of film.

But as Caliban arises from cannibal, By Lacan arises necessarily from Caliban, is its perpetuation or transformation. Ariel is the *letrado* or the man of letters—the gender inflection is intended—whose chosen métier is literature and/or the essay. Caliban, if s/he in fact is meant to designate a new, postcolonial Latin American subject, is interpellated culturally today, however, not by literature but by the mass media. S/he works perhaps as a TV technician, like the husband in the Cuban film *Portrait of Teresa*. It is not that s/he is necessarily indifferent to literature—the husband liked the sort of counterespionage novel popular in Cuba in the early years of the Revolution—but, as opposed to the "traditional intellectual," to recall Gramsci's concept, literature is not his or her primary cultural referent.

The problem is that Latin American left cultural politics is still founded on a model of cultural authority and pedagogy in which, as we have just noted, literature is positioned as the discourse that is crucially formative of Latin American identity and possibility. Latin American neoconservatives, like the Venezuelan Carlos Rangel, have denounced this as a kind of cultural Arielism, in which literature itself and/or the humanistic values it connotes are articulated as ideological signifiers of anti-imperialism and anti-U.S.-style modernization.

What happens if we replace this high-minded literary idealism with something like U.S. mass culture as a model for the cultural politics of the Latin American left? (This is in essence what happens with the notion and practice of a Latin American postmodernism, which I take up in part III.) I want to be clear here: I am not proposing as a model U.S. mass culture as such, but rather the possibilities of production, distribution, and consumption that it represents or suggests. Assume, for example, the following imaginary, but certainly *imaginable*, situation: a photo of a young combatant of the Salvadoran FMLN wearing a Madonna T-shirt. A kind of cultural criticism identified with the Frankfurt School and dependency theory with which we all are familiar (and in some cases may even have practiced) would speak about how this person had become a revolutionary *in spite of* the cultural imperialism represented by the T-shirt and exported U.S. pop culture generally. I'll come back to the problem of cultural imperialism in a moment, but I want to ask now if there is some way in which the identification of the young person with Madonna, instead of complicating the development of a revolutionary consciousness and militancy, might not in fact stimulate it. I'm thinking here of two things: one is a statement by one of the comandantes of the FMLN, who noted that rock music (the Beatles and so on) had been precisely one of the formative musics of his adolescence, that he shared this experience with the corresponding generation in the United States; the other is *Rodrigo D: No Future*, the extraordinary Colombian film directed by Victor Gaviria about punk rockers in the slums of Medellín. It would be difficult to see *Rodrigo D* and continue to talk about rock as a form of cultural imperialism; it is, rather, a way that the young people shown in the film live culturally their experience of proletarianization and alienation.

This is not to say that a young person identified with the right, or a member of a death squad, could not also be a Madonna fan. A Madonna video on the South Florida-based TV Martí that is funded by the U.S. government to destabilize Cuba would be an act of cultural imperialism, one appropriately resisted by the Cuban government's jamming of the transmission and by U.S. citizens protesting the use of their tax dollars to subsidize the station. The same video, broadcast on Cuban television as part of its regular programming, would be another thing altogether. It is not the Madonna video as such that is problematic—Cuba already buys a considerable amount of U.S.-produced TV material (from, among others, Ted Turner) and would buy more except for the blockade—but rather its context of transmission. To paraphrase something Ernesto Laclau noted in a different—but not entirely unrelated—context: the ideological connotation of the Madonna video comes not so much from its *content* as from its *form* of articulation as a cultural signifier.

One possible move away from the unhappy marriage in Latin American cultural studies of Frankfurt School critique and dependency theory would be a rejection of the behaviorism implicit in it in favor of an exploration of the possibility of a differential Latin American or third world reception of imported and/or imposed U.S. culture, whether this be high-, low-, or middlebrow. This is of course something close to the party line of film and media studies, and at the same time a variant of the way in which Latin American literary history sees the European Baroque as being transformed—the Brazilians like the metaphor of cultural "cannibalism" (*antropofagia*)—into the cultural instrument of an emerging creole consciousness in the colony. Nelson Osorio, responding to my point about the role of rock in Latin America youth culture, observes:

> They change the brand names, they change the license plates on their cars and they turn them into something else. I think this is the most interesting process going on in Latin America today. Not the inevitable—up to now—importation of elements of ideological consumption, but the way in which these are refunctioned and converted into something else.[8]

Yes and no. Because, as *Rodrigo D: No Future* shows, punk rock already is "something else" without the need to be "refunctioned and converted." The difference between the slum kids of Medellín who consume punk rock and the unemployed British working-class youth on the dole who invented it is not all that significant in class (or linguistic or musical) terms. They are both part of a postfordist, transnational subproletariat in formation. Moreover, even in the United States the kind of popular culture represented by rock in general is ideologically and socially very heterogeneous. It stems from subaltern social groups: poor whites, African-Americans, Jews, Italians, Latinos (Richie Valens, Los Lobos, and so on). Although it is certainly a form of capitalist culture, unlike even progressive forms of literature, it is created neither by nor for members of the ruling class. Even in its most commercial forms it retains a popular character, distinct from the official culture of the ruling class (although it can be, and obviously has been, articulated ideologically as a signifier of imperialism, as in the case of the successful promotion of jazz by the State Department as part of its anticommunist propaganda campaign in the fifties).

Moreover, the notion of a *differential* appropriation of international mass culture that underlies Osorio's remark is precisely something that postmodernist theory puts into question, because it implies a distanced and ironic form of reception; that is, a reception essentially by intellectuals of the traditional type. Baudrillard's comment in *In the Shadow of the Silent Majorities* is characteristically overstated, but perhaps relevant here:

> In the case of the media, traditional resistance consists of reinterpreting messages according to the group's own code and for its own ends. The masses, on the contrary, accept everything and redirect everything *en bloc* into the spectacular, without requiring any other code, without requiring any meaning, ultimately without resistance, but making everything slide into an indeterminate sphere which is not even that of non-sense, but that of overall manipulation/ fascination.[9]

If, however, we agree that the decisive terrain of ideological struggle in the contemporary world is the mass media, have we not in a certain sense ceded the victory to the enemy from the start? That would seem to be the basis of Baudrillard's pessimism and quietism. But consider for a moment what would seem on the face of it to be the opposite of the highly commodified cultural system of manipulation/fascination represented by U.S. mass culture: the cultural politics of "actually existing socialism." It goes without saying that the crisis of this system was in some crucial way a cultural crisis. I would venture the thought, however, that the cultural problems of actually existing socialism did not happen at the level of high culture. Despite all the well-known problems of censorship, bureaucracy, and so on, there exists or existed a more or less adequate high culture in the socialist countries (think of Brecht, Eisler, or Christa Wolf in East Germany, to give only one example). The problems happened rather at the level of the efforts to create a socialist mass or pop culture under the direction of Communist parties whose members tended to share a humanistic overvalorization of the literary. The socialist countries were not and are not able to compete effectively with capitalism in the creation of mass culture. In relation to this problem, and for our purposes here, the great debates that framed left cultural discussion for so many decades—between, for example, modernism and realism, Brecht and Lukács, Adorno and Benjamin, the Gang of Four and the capitalist roaders over the Peking Opera, Cortázar and Oscar Collazos over the Latin American novel—are not all that relevant. Stalinist socialist realism as much as the sort of left modernism defended by Trotskyists, the grass-roots poetry workshop movement sponsored by Ernesto Cardenal in Nicaragua as much as the more cosmopolitan and professionalized literary model defended by Rosario Murillo and the journal *Ventana*, represent normative and pedagogic principles of cultural activity, based in Latin America on a prolongation of Rama's "ciudad letrada." The contending positions propose to correct in one way or another—alienation effects in the case of modernism, identification in the case of socialist realism—what is seen as the false or degraded consciousness of cultural consumers from the popular classes.

But this is not in essence a position all that different from that of nineteenth-century liberals like Sarmiento or Bello, who saw in the standardization of language and culture represented by written literature the antidote to the continent's barbarism or cultural adolescence. The actual cultural policies that tend to accompany these literary debates, like the literacy campaigns in Cuba or Nicaragua, undoubtedly change the nature of the relation between Ariel and Caliban by giving the power of literacy to broader sectors of the population; but they also reinscribe it by making literature and literacy again the privileged signifiers of cultural authority.

The Puerto Rican critic Julio Ramos has undertaken in his book on José Martí an anatomy of what he terms—against Octavio Paz's idea of literature as a "compensatory modernity" for Latin America's failure to modernize at the political or economic level—the complicity of literature and modernization.[10] For Ramos, the *modernista* movement at the turn of the century implied the disintegration of the "republic of letters"—the association of literature and the founding of the nation-state—represented by figures like Bello or Sarmiento. But if, in writers like Darío and Martí, literature is no longer seen as the language of the state, if in fact it feeds on precisely the opposition to the processes of rationalization represented by the state and the public sphere, it also claims the authority of being an integrative, totalizing discourse in a context of the "disassociation of sensibility" imposed on traditional elites by a sudden and chaotic experience of modernity.

In general terms, the ideology of the *modernista* writers—and they were the founders of modern Latin American literature—involved the opposition of the aesthetic as such—seen as the essence of Latin American identity itself—to the activities and scientific and pedagogic discourses (positivism, naturalism, utilitarianism, behaviorism, Taylorism, etc.) of modernity. For the *modernistas*, Ramos suggests, the writer is "a properly *modern* hero precisely because his effort to synthesize discursive roles and functions presupposes the antitheses generated by the division of labor and the fragmentation of the relatively integrated public sphere in which the writing of the *letrados* had operated" (14).

The experience of an imperialist modernity in Latin America involved not only the alienations of business and technology for the traditional elites, represented by intellectuals like Rodó. It brought with it also the problem of coming to terms with a growing proletariat and urban popular classes.

Ramos discovers (as a response to this problem, and at the same time as a compensation for the danger that the aesthetic autonomy sought by the *modernistas* implied literature's ineffectiveness as a public discourse) an emerging articulation of the humanities and the university by essayists—and precisely *in* the essay as a form—like Rodó, Martí, Hostos, Alfonso Reyes, Ricardo Rojas, Pedro Henríquez Ureña, or Vasconcelos. Through their pedagogic institutionalization of literature, these writers "refunctionalize literary rhetorics as paradigms against the social chaos and massification, claiming for the humanities a normative role of administration and control in a world where a new form of barbarism proliferated: the proletarian 'masses' " (216). Through its very questioning of a modernization imposed from abroad, *modernista* literature could "nourish and at the same time nourish itself from the emerging nationalism and Latin Americanism of the era, both based in cultural discourses which the literary field generated" (221).

Martí's famous essay "Nuestra América," which Retamar saw as the very essence of a Calibanesque project in Latin American culture, is instead for Ramos an example of this new Americanist ideology of literature and the humanities. It inverts the relation of subordination between intellectual and people, writing and orality in Sarmiento or Bello, making the indigenous and subaltern the basis of Latin American identity. But at the same time, its own stylistic will to power as an essay denounces a sense of the literary as both the adequate and the *necessary* form of expression of Latin Americanism. (Martí evokes the image of "masas mudas de indios"—mute masses of Indians.) This sense of a properly literary form of civic heroism institutes a new relation between literature and power. It is a question, Ramos concludes, "of an aestheticization of politics which postulates the indispensable role of literary knowledge in the administration of good government" (243).

What deconstructs the nineteenth-century republic of letters and the traditional role of the writer as national patriarch for Martí is precisely his experience of New York and of the possibilities of mass spectacle and entertainment that it offered. It is no accident, in this sense, that the key article of Martí for Ramos is "Coney Island," from his *Escenas norteamericanas*, where the writer (who lived for many years in New York) describes ambivalently his experience of U.S. mass culture and "entertainment."

In situations of uneven development where one form or another of precapitalist cultural elitism defined by a marked separation between intellectuals and the popular sectors has prevailed (among these could be counted the situation of intellectuals in most socialist countries), the commodification of cultural production through the operation of the market and through new technologies of mass culture can be—particularly in combination with an expansion of the system of public education at all levels and a rise in the standard of living of the population as a whole—an effective means of cultural democratization and redistribution of cultural use-values and commodities, allowing not only new modes of cultural consumption but also an increased access to the means of cultural production by subaltern groups and classes. By contrast, we can observe in the cultural policies undertaken by the Soviet model of socialism the persistence of an ideology of the literary, which, apart from conjunctural differences, maintains a close affinity with bourgeois humanism and, in the case of socialist regimes in the Third World, with colonial or neocolonial cultural castes. As Althusser demonstrated, this ideology is combined in Stalinism with a mechanical idea of the development of the forces of production and a consequent political economy of socialist primitive accumulation, which entails a coercive action by the state and the party on the masses, and which in turn leads to their gradual alienation from the socialist project itself.

One of the obvious consequences of the decentering of literature that the discussion above proposes would be cultural studies, to which, via a detour through testimonio, I now turn. As many readers are aware, the New Right made of *I, Rigoberta Menchú: An Indian Woman in Guatemala*—the English version of perhaps the most well-known testimonial narrative of the 1980s in Latin America—a special target of its attacks on multiculturalism and political correctness in the humanities. I am thinking here particularly of Dinesh

D'Souza's *Illiberal Education*, with its chapter "Travels with Rigoberta" on the debate over the Stanford undergraduate general education requirement, in which the then secretary of education for the Reagan administration, William Bennett, intervened directly. From there the topic of Rigoberta Menchú and her famous testimonio passed into the pages of the *Atlantic Monthly*, the *Wall Street Journal*, *Newsweek*, the *New York Review of Books*, and so on, feeding into a media blitz on the multiculturalism debate that continues today with the award of the Nobel Peace Prize to Menchú in 1992.[11]

Perhaps better than the left, still mired in a habitual bad faith about university life and intellectuals, the cultural commissars of the New Right like D'Souza understood that the university is a crucial institution of contemporary society. They shared with their adversary in the multiculturalism debate—which was not the left but the present generation of "liberal" university and college administrators—something like the following ensemble of issues:

new forms of public policy entailed by the need to administer and discipline an increasingly multicultural U.S. population and a transnational proletariat imposed by the current processes of globalization of capital and corresponding demographic shifts;

the central role of the university (as itself an eminently "transnational" institution) in relation to this project, particularly in the interface it offers between public policy, area studies, and postmodernist theory and pedagogy;

the recognition that, for better or worse, large parts of the university, particularly in the humanities, are significantly impacted, if not dominated by what for short we can call the generation of the "sixties";

the problems caused for public policy by the imcomprehension or misunderstanding of subaltern social groups by previously dominant academic methodologies and disciplines (the failure of U.S. policy in the Vietnam War—a policy generated in large part out of the social sciences—was one of the first indications of this);

the phenomenon of deterritorialization—above all, the new permeability of frontiers—and its economic, demographic, linguistic, and cultural consequences;

the displacement in the humanities, as a consequence of all of the above, of the traditional program of literature, fine arts, and philosophy, by huge communications programs, courses on film, TV, and popular culture, and the new interfaces betwen humanities and social sciences: in brief, the emergence of cultural studies.

Given the anxiety shown by the defenders of the traditional literary curriculum over the dissemination of a text like *I, Rigoberta Menchú*, it should not surprise us that its narrator declares herself in effect a postmodernist and a practitioner of "theoretical antihumanism." Rigoberta Menchú is fond of saying things like:

> They have tried to take our things away and impose others on us, be it through religion, through dividing up the land, through schools, through books, through radio, through all things modern. (170–71)

Or:

> For the Indian, it is better not to study than to become like *ladinos*. (205)

We will come back to this curious resistance to literacy and education in part II. For now it is enough to note that Menchú *uses* the possibility of producing a text already established as a literary and ethnographic genre to address a reading public constituted in large part by university-educated people, without succumbing to an ideology of the literary generated and maintained by the university, or, what amounts to the same thing, without abandoning her identity as a member of her community.

Anticipating a subsequent discussion, I would like to contrast this posture briefly with the strategy represented by autobiography, where the possibility and act of producing a literary text—writing your "life"—entail precisely the abandonment of a "traditional" identity in favor of the sort of secularized and mobile individualism represented by the "author." The contemporary case that is most relevant here is a text that, in direct contrast to *I, Rigoberta Menchú*, was much admired by the New Right because of its critique of bilingual education. I refer, of course, to Richard Rodriguez's "middleclass pastoral," *Hunger of Memory*,[12] which tells the story of the education and upward mobility of a Chicano child, a process that eventually involves the loss not only of his ethnic identification, but also of his name. Richard Rodriguez had begun his life as Ricardo Rodríguez (*with* the accent), the child of Mexican parents in a working-class neighborhood of Sacramento. "Once upon a time I was a 'socially-disadvantaged' child," he writes. "Thirty years later I write this book as a middle-class American. Assimilated" (3).

For Rodriguez, the public language of authority and power in the United States is English. Spanish is the language of the private sphere of the home and the family. The "law of the father," which imposes the symbolic castration necessary for his accesion to full citizenship, is in effect the requirement to abandon Spanish. Rodriguez's education and literary apprenticeship—thanks to scholarships to Stanford and then Berkeley, where he specializes in English Renaissance literature—are homologous with the passage from the Imaginary to the Symbolic in the Lacanian scheme of subject formation. Returning to his old neighborhood from the university one summer to take a construction job, he observes of his Spanish-speaking fellow workers:

> Their silence is more telling. They lack a public identity. They remain profoundly alien. . . . I had finally come face to face with *los pobres*. (138–39)

I know of no more exact description of the social production of a sense of the subaltern as other and of the implication of the university and literature in this act. Spivak's famous question, "Can the subaltern speak?," and her answer—against the grain of our inclination to identify the subaltern precisely with speech—that it cannot, not as such (because "the subaltern is the name of a place which is so displaced that to make it speak would be like the arrival of Godot on a bus")[13] were meant to show in the posture of good faith of the politically correct academic or the solidarity activist the trace of the colonial literary construction of a third world other who can speak with us, thereby smoothing over any anxiety about the reality of difference and antagonism that a silence might have provoked, and affirming the ethical integrity of our subject position. Richard Rodriguez can speak (write) eloquently in English to an Anglo, college-educated reading public of the need for the assimilation of Latinos like himself into what he regards as the dominant culture of a country that, with a Spanish-surnamed (and largely Spanish-speaking) population of some twenty-five million, is today the fourth or fifth largest in the Hispanic world. Rodriguez can speak, in other words, but not as a subaltern, not as Ricardo Rodríguez, and not in Spanish.

Perhaps the most interesting aspect of testimonio in this respect is that it offers both a model and a concrete practice of new forms of solidarity between college-educated intellectuals like Richard Rodriguez and subaltern communities and classes. It offers also, as in the case of Rigoberta Menchú herself, a new, deterritorialized, organic intellectual of the subaltern, capable of acting effectively in global circuits of power and representation. Testimonio appears on the scene in the context of the crisis of the representativity of traditional political parties and projects of the left. Its sociopolitical correlative tends to be "new social movements" like the organization of the Mothers of the Disappeared, Menchú's own CUC (Committee of Campesino Unity), the base communities of liberation theology, solidarity and human-rights networks: movements, in other words, that stress a "micropolitics" of rights and identity and that use testimonial practices in their social protagonism (as in the slogan of the AIDS activist group ACT UP "Silence = Death").

We could contrast the kind of politics that testimonio both models and enacts with the vision of cultural agency and representation associated with communism. Many readers will be familiar with the conclusion of "The Heights of Machu Picchu" in Pablo Neruda's epic poem of Latin American history, *Canto General* (General Song, 1947). Abandoning the description of the city and its spectacular setting, Neruda's voice invites its dead inhabitants, and by extension the masses of Latin America, silenced and forgotten in centuries of colonial rule, to "rise and be born with me" ("Sube a nacer conmigo"):

Yo vengo a hablar por vuestra boca muerta
A través de toda la tierra juntad todos
los silenciosos labios derramados
y desde el fondo habladme toda esta larga noche,
como yo estuviera con vosotros anclado,
contadme todo, cadena a cadena

....

Acudid a mis venas y a mi boca
Hablad por mis palabras y mi sangre.

[I come to speak through your dead mouth / From all over the face of the earth bring together all / the silent lips scattered there / and from the depths speak to me this long night / as if I were anchored with you / tell me all, chain by chain. / . . . Come to my veins and to my mouth / Speak through my words and my blood.]

Neruda's invitation offers a vertical model of representation (in the double sense of mimesis and political representation) and of the relation between progressive intellectuals and the popular masses of past and present Latin American society. Neruda speaks for the people, as a "tribune of the people"— to recall the Bolshevik concept; but it is not the people itself that speaks, the "mute masses of Indians," in Martí's phrase. In fact, in Neruda's invocation the people as such is dead ("boca muerta"), buried in the ruins of the empty city it built and in the muteness of its own unrecorded history, from which only the voice of the poet can redeem it. This figuration of the relation between literature and subalternity recalls the paradox that Benjamin identified in the Baroque *Trauerspiel*: the process of sublimation of something generated by its representation in writing at the same time traces the imminence of death and decay. "Significance and death both come to fruition in historical development, just as they are closely linked in the creature's graceless state of sin."[14]

It is not my intention to denigrate Neruda or the often exemplary historical protagonism of the Chilean Communist party here. But it seems to me that this model of representation no longer functions, that we find ourselves precisely in the midst of its catachresis, a catachresis that is not so much the crisis of Marxism as such but of the persistence within Marxism of bourgeois-humanist concepts of history and social protagonism. We could substitute the position of enunciation in Neruda's poem for our position, the position of literary criticism and literary intellectuals in relation to not only the subaltern but also the otherness of literature itself (in the sense that literature "speaks" through us its meaning and significance). What happens if we replace this vertical position of enunciation with a horizontal one, that is, if we (1) at least question the situation of structural privilege that the history of sexism, colonialism, and imperialism confers on us, and (2) begin to enter into direct relation with the forms of political agency of subaltern social groups? Such a shift—and I do not minimize the difficulties of accomplishing it—would, in the current slogan, move us "beyond the politics of representation" to a model of teaching and criticism that would see these as forms of solidarity practice.

Feminism provides a good example of what I have in mind. Academic feminist theory and criticism do not just "represent" a political-legal practice that happens essentially outside the university; the contemporary women's movement *passes through* the university and the school system. The kind of theoretical work someone like Catharine Mac-Kinnon does on women and law has immediate consequences for organizations struggling at both the local and international level for women's rights. It can, as in the area of sexual harassment described in Anita Hill's testimony, even create legal rights and entitlements that did not previously exist. In the emerging global society, based on the control and manipulation of information and images and the production of newly skilled forms of labor power, our location within the educational apparatus acquires a new and unexpected power of agency. Hence the anxiety of the New Right ideologues about the proliferation of "theory" in higher education.

I want to end by returning to our immediate field of action and effectiveness, in particular to the question of cultural studies as an alternative to the traditional "literary" curriculum of the humanities. Michael Nerlich has argued, against the tendency to polarize popular and elite culture, that "Watching television or a football game; going jogging, to the theater, or to a party; listening to the Beatles and Ligetti; singing *Auprès de ma blonde* or *Lo tiré al pozo* and reading Beckett or Mallarmé, watching an erotic movie, and looking at paintings by Michelangelo or Kandinsky or Pollock or Giotto di Bondone (etc., etc.) . . . are not contradictory or concurrent activities, but rather complementary ones."[15] This is true, but it is true *for us*. And mass culture is not exactly subaltern culture; apart from transitional and intermediate forms like the testimonio, the manifestations of subaltern culture have in general only an "anthropolgical" value for us. Either we do not have direct access to them (their presentation is mediated precisely by literature, music, ethnographic documentaries, and so on), or they are reified in the process of information retrieval involved in their study by this or that academic discipline (I insist again on the role of the university and cultural institutions like museums in *making* things subaltern, as in the case of Richard Rodriguez's "education").

In spite of its characteristic appeal to the local and everyday, to *petites histoires* rather than *grands récits*, there is a kind of aesthetic utopianism in the celebration of popular culture or mass culture that has been a central strand of cultural studies from Thompson's *The Making of the English Working Class* to the current idealization of Madonna as a poststructuralist heroine. There is the danger that such a celebration (which I have both shared and protagonized, as the reader may gather from my own earlier remarks on Madonna or the discussion of postmodern music in chapter 7) may involve simply a new variation of the ideology of the literary, via the displacement of a modernist program from the sphere of high culture to the popular, now seen as more aesthetically dynamic and effective (as if the shift from high to low were something like the equivalent of the formalist principle of estrangement or *ostranenie*, with the end result being the production of something like a pop sublime). Lyotard himself has noted that postmodernism in its desire to be ruptural and "new" is an extension of the modernist ideology that it supposedly displaces.

To the extent that mass or popular culture can be reaestheticized, it is possible for the social and natural sciences to regroup around a (Kantian) rearticulation of disciplinary specificities, which neutralizes the way in which, in its inception, cultural studies was a direct challenge (and alternative) to what they were doing. The fact/value distinction, which previously regulated the separation of the humanities from the sciences and which it was the main challenge of "theory" to weaken, can now be reinscribed within cultural studies itself. In such an articulation of the field, the relation between humanities and social and natural sciences becomes dialogical, in the sense that they can "learn" from each other. But the point of cultural studies was not so much to create a dialogue between disciplines as to challenge the integrity of disciplinary boundaries per se, "infiltrating" into them—the metaphor is Gayatri Spivak's—a *trans-* rather than interdisciplinary practice, whose models were Marxism, feminism, structuralism, and deconstruction (cultural studies was in a sense the consequence of the incidence of these discourses—and of mass culture itself—in the human sciences).[16] Even as the struggle to institutionalize cultural studies is still going on in many places, the likelihood is that it will be naturalized in the curriculum and begin to approximate something like an epistemological (and elite) "Faculty Club," rather than a way of carrying into the academy issues of class struggle, decolonization, antiracism, women's liberation, and the like.

As I argue in my remarks on Stephen Greenblatt and the new historicism in chapter 2, the institutionalization of cultural studies (and, in a related way, of a multicultural curriculum) is more or less compatible with a revision of the forms of academic knowledge in and around the humanities demanded by the present stage of capitalism (however one chooses to characterize it). In fact, it may well be that the "liberals" have already won the debate, and that multiculturalism and cultural studies are being prepared as the places for a redefinition of educational curricula and disciplinary structures in the period ahead. The conversion of cultural studies from a form of radical opposition to the avant-garde of bourgeois hegemony will be driven by three major concerns: (1) making cultural studies acceptable to faculty, administrators, and trustees rather than to students (we may expect the usual quota of "required" courses, whereas cultural studies in its inception aimed to liberate students from disciplinary requirements by allowing them to vote with their feet, so to speak); (2) diluting its potential to become a form of ideological-epistemological agency of the social groups and movements outside the university whose subalternity it is precisely concerned with theorizing; (3) keeping cultural studies separate from the natural sciences and the sphere of technology and the professional schools.

The key moves in this respect will be to detach cultural studies from its "centering" in discourses like Marxism or feminism that imply both the inadequacy of existing forms of academic disciplinarity and the need for structural transformation of the existing social relations. The code words of this project will be "pluralism" and "interdisciplinarity," but the end effect will be depoliticization. (This is in fact more or less what, after seven years of operation, has happened to the graduate program in cultural studies that Gayatri Spivak and I were involved in forming at the University of Pittsburgh.) I believe it is still worth making the struggle for (and in) cultural studies, but just at the moment when its presence in the contemporary university seems assured, cultural studies has begun to lose the radicalizing force that accompanied its emergence as a field (the New Right was not wrong in its intuition that things like cultural studies involved a continuation of the radical project of the sixties within higher education).[17]

Instead of cultural studies, then, the nature of the project I am proposing here is closer in aim, if not in method, to the "theoretical antihumanism" of Althusser that I invoked earlier apropos the stance of Rigoberta Menchú in her testimonio. The slogans "Against Literature" and "By Lacan" suggest not so much the supplantation of literature as a more agnostic posture toward it, a way of problematizing it in the very act of teaching it in its disciplinary location. (By the same token, cultural studies, which seemed to be the pedagogic embodiment of something like a critical materialism, now needs itself to be interrogated in the same spirit.)

I do not have many illusions about the pedagogic viability of such a project. The temptation is always to recur to some variation or other of the strategy outlined in the passage from Spivak at the beginning of this chapter: to use literature, in other words, as a way to bring to the attention of our students (or ourselves) how race, class, and gender oppression are constructed. But is this not like the social-democratic illusion that the existing state apparatus, in the hands of "good" people who "represent" popular interests, can cease to function as a machinery of exploitation and oppression? Can you have fundamental social change without changing the forms of the state? Can you have fundamental social change without changing the forms of literature (this is the question that introduces the discussion of testimonio in part II)?

In a situation where not only our professional lives but also our very sense of ourselves as good and caring people is existentially linked in some way with literature, I understand that no reader of these words is going to give up easily the beliefs and tasks to which s/he has dedicated his or her life. What I do think is possible, however, is a relative democratization of our field via, among other things, the development of a radically historicized concept of literature.[18] But if this were to happen, how could literature continue to distinguish itself from its nonliterary other? What happens when it recognizes itself as simply one discourse among many? Can the distinction between teleological and aesthetic judgment that is at the heart of formalism and of the disciplinary separation between "culture" and the sciences be transgressed? The answer to these questions should be the task of what, in the spirit of the title to this chapter, I would propose to call a *psychoanalysis of literature*. As in any psychoanalysis, it is not a matter of liquidating the subject (in spite of its own anxious fantasies), nor of curing it once and for all, but simply of reforming it on new bases so as to make it somewhat more capable of solidarity and love.

Part I
In Literature

CHAPTER 2

The Formation of the Ideology of the Literary (from Garcilaso to Greenblatt)

W e tend to think of literature as a sanctioned space for the expression of social dissidence or marginality. That is probably why many of us were attracted to it in the first place. My indoctrination into literature, for example, was through the writers of the American Beat Generation of the fifties and early sixties, who mirrored my own adolescent anger and rebelliousness. Something similar, perhaps, happens today with deconstruction or poststructuralist criticism, which show the play of difference and possibility concealed by the text's illusion of mastery and closure.

But literature has not always had this "dissident" or oppositional character. As McLuhan suggested in his famous thesis, the fusion of written literature with the technology of movable type was in fact one of the conditions of possibility for the emergence of the modern European state itself, and vice versa. This does not imply that literature was ideologically homogenous: neither were the post-Renaissance nation-states or their colonial empires ideologically homogenous. Hegemony—this was, after all, Gramsci's point—is founded on the incorporation and neutralization of contradictions, not on a purely monological discourse. In what amounts to a rebuttal of a simpleminded Bakhtinianism, Wlad Godzich has observed that even a text as evidently "dialogical" in its construction as *Don Quijote* presumed in its own time an ideal reader that was in a sense the absolutist state itself, because it was only from the panoptic perspective of the state—itself founded, like the novel, on the elaboration and imposition of a single national language— 25 that each of the text's multiple discourses could be seen and evaluated. Difference could be tolerated—even encouraged—but only within the centralized power system represented by the state and a national language, which existed, like the literary text itself, both to make difference possible and to contain it.[1]

In her study of literary education in colonial India, *Masks of Conquest*, Gauri Viswanathan offers a striking extension of the paradox that Godzich suggests. She notes "the irony that English literature appeared as a subject in the curriculum of the colonies long before it was institutionalized in the home country. As early as the 1820s, when the classical curriculum still reigned supreme in England despite the strenuous efforts of some concerned critics to loosen its hold, English as the study of culture and not simply the study of language had already found a secure place in the British Indian curriculum." "The history of education in British India shows," Viswanathan continues, "that certain humanistic functions traditionally associated with literature—for example, the shaping of character or the development of the aesthetic sense or the disciplines of ethical thinking—were considered essential to the processes of sociopolitical control by the guardians of the same tradition."[2]

But why? "If indeed the British were the unchallenged military power of India, . . . what accounts for (their) readiness to turn to a disciplinary branch of knowledge to perform the task of administering their colonial subjects?" (10). Viswanathan replies that the use of English literature in the colonial curriculum was less the result of an uncontested cultural ethnocentrism that was simply imposed; it responded rather to the British sense of the *vulnerability* of their authority. It "was less a statement of the superiority of the West than a vital, active instrument of Western hegemony in concert with commercial expansion and military action" (166–67). Literature provided the British with a way of negotiating the contradictions internal to their own project between Parliament, the missionaries, and the East India Company, between the colonial administration and the Indian elites in their various caste and sectarian configurations, and between these elites in turn (who above their ethnic and religious differences could share through English literature a common model of cultural excellence and ethical superiority) and the Indian subaltern classes. What allowed it to play this mediating function in the colonies was precisely its *distance* as a "modern," secularized cultural practice from religious dogma and traditional cultures. The consequence (and here Viswanathan's work intersects with the critique of nationalism made by the Subaltern Studies Group) was a Westernization, in effect, of even the subsequent forms of Indian nationalism, which have to pass through the discursive filter of English literature.[3]

Given the British policy of religious neutrality in its colonies and the evident difference in phase—Viswanathan is concerned with nineteenth-century India—the situation she describes is not exactly that of colonial Latin America. But it does help us understand that paradoxical phenomenon which is at the heart of the Spanish Baroque: Gongorism, resisted and denounced as heretical in the metropolis (the Inquisition prohibited the sale of the first commercial edition of Góngora's poetry in 1627), becomes in the colonies a quasi-official aesthetic manner for more than a century and continues to be celebrated even today as a marker of Latin American cultural identity (I will return to these matters in chapter 3).

If we extrapolate from Viswanathan's account, literature as such was one of the instruments of European colonial rule (and by extension is implicated in the contemporary structure of neocolonial and imperialist control). No doubt in Latin America, as in nineteenth-century India (under admittedly very different circumstances), literature, precisely because of its centrality in the colonial apparatus, was also a cultural practice through which, by a process of differential reception, manipulation, refunctioning, parody, and the like, forms of creole separatism and eventually nationalism could incubate, particularly among the elites most affected by literary study. But there, from the point of view of the subaltern classes that constituted the vast majority of the population of both regions, and given in particular the noncorrespondence between their interests and the "nationalist" culture and state forms created by these elites, is precisely the problem.

It is from this vantage point that I want to consider one of the founding texts of Spanish and Latin American literary modernity, Garcilaso de la Vega's sonnet 23, "En tanto que de rosa y azucena" (While the colors of the rose and the lily), written around 1525 and first published in the edition of his poems prepared by his friend Boscán around 1540. Garcilaso is credited in Spanish literary history with making the lyric forms developed in Italy by Petrarch and his successors in the fifteenth century work as poetry in Castilian, which under both the Catholic Kings and Charles V, the first Spanish Hapsburg, was being promoted and/or imposed as the language of both national consolidation and colonial expansion.

I make the connection between these facts of power and sonnet 23 (which is a love poem) circumstantially via Cervantes's short novel *El licenciado Vidriera* (c. 1602), usually translated as Bachelor (in the academic sense) Glass, punning in English as in Spanish between the name of the thing and the surname of a person. The hero, Tomás, is a young man from an unspecified, but apparently lower-class, background who has managed through the patronage of two aristocrats who befriend him to obtain a degree at the University of Salamanca, the most prestigious Spanish university of the day. On graduating, he leaves for Italy on what was the Golden Age equivalent of "study abroad," taking two books with him: a breviary and a "Garcilaso sin comento" (without, that is, the "learned" commentaries of El Brocense or Herrera, the two major canonizers of Garcilaso's poetry in the Renaissance). Hapsburg imperialism had many dimensions, and Cervantes's own, like his hero's, was the Mediterranean. But it is easy to imagine a similar detail in the case of a young university graduate about to embark for the New World. (Cervantes himself thought of emigrating to America as a solution to his numerous financial problems, and his contemporary and rival Mateo Alemán, author of the most popular novel in both Spain and Latin America in the seventeenth century, the picaresque *Guzmán de Alfarache*, actually did emigrate to the colonies.) Some seventy years earlier, Garcilaso himself had been a courtier in the retinue of Charles V. As such he probably supported and participated in the repression of Spain's version of the Peasant Revolts, the rebellions of the *comunidades* in the 1520s, and he was killed in battle at a young age defending Spanish positions in France.

But surely things like Petrarchan sonnets belong to the "private sphere," and it was the job of *epic* (or the historical chronicle or essay, the sermon, the legal-theological tract) to constitute the discourse of empire. Roland Greene has proposed, nevertheless, that "the international appeal of Petrarchism in the sixteenth century is largely political, or to be more specific, colonial." He writes:

> [Because] of its engagement with such political issues as the distribution of power among agents, the assimilation of difference, and the organization of individual desires into common structures of action and reaction, Petrarchan subjectivity finds a new immediacy in Europe's discovery and colonization of the New World. I would go even further, past merely explaining the fashion for this mode of amatory poetry in the period, and argue that in the first phase of colonization, until 1600, Petrarchism operates as the original colonial discourse in the Americas, the first highly conventional language brought over from Europe that adequately expresses colonial experience as a set of relations between individual standpoints, that treats the frustrations as well as the ambitions of Europeans, and that allows Americans the capacity to play out their role as unwilling (or at most deeply ambivalent) participants in someone else's enterprise. . . . In the widest sense, I mean to suggest that Petrarchan ideologies and discursive structures are part of the foundation of American, especially Latin American, literatures and cultures, that even after 1600 Petrarchism and the relations articulated by it survive as a latent but indissoluble bond between the Europeans and their colonized peoples in such places as Mexico, Peru, Brazil, and—to a lesser extent—the United States.[4]

What Greene's point obliges us to understand is not so much the *representation* of the colonial enterprise in Renaissance literature as the way in which literature of any sort was a condition for the formation of the subject-form of the colonial elites. Tomás in Cervantes's novel is a *letrado* or "man of letters," meaning in practice both a university graduate—a *licenciado*—and, as the name suggests, an almost always masculine subject formed *by* and to some extent *for* literature (in Renaissance Spanish, *letras*). In early modern

Europe literature and the university—particularly the humanities—are closely linked. This is not the case—as it may sometimes seem today—of the humanities incorporating and legislating a literary production that happens essentially outside the university; as an institution of Renaissance society, literature is itself a product of the humanities, grows up inside them (something clearly evident in the first classic of modern Spanish literature, *La Celestina*, which had its origins in a classroom exercise called the *comedia humanística*). Moreover, as Richard Kagan has shown, the cycle of rise and decline of Spanish universities in the Golden Age was closely related to the rise and decline of the Spanish empire itself.[5] In the late sixteenth century, beginning perhaps with the Italian Mannerists and extending into the Baroque, a split emerges between university-based literary theory and the actual practice of writers, but it remains the case that on the whole these writers, and their audiences, are university-trained.

The general tendency in European historiography has been to represent Renaissance humanism and the new literary forms and exercises it championed as a consequence of the Nominalist critique of Scholasticism and the related emergence of a secular, urban bourgeois culture: to see modern literature, in other words, as a historically progressive or protoliberal cultural form. One would be hard put to deny this: it is, after all, a commonplace that the modern novel is not only a reflection of the emerging brave new world of a society based increasingly on market exchange and capitalism, but also one of the central ideological practices by which bourgeois-democratic culture is constituted as such, in a process of protracted cultural revolution that led to the displacement of the authority of religion and oral narrative by literature.

But, as Paul Otto Kristeller pointed out in his Oberlin lectures on Renaissance humanism, this vision of literature and humanism is itself a product of the way liberal historicism constructs the Renaissance as an epoch (as the awakening of the modern "individual" and of modernity itself). It is true, Kristeller noted, that the humanists attacked Scholasticism and the authority of Aristotle and religious dogma, but they also opposed the developments that would lead to the development of modern science and natural philosophy.[6]

Not only were the humanists on the wrong side of many of the great debates about science, they were also—despite their commitment to new forms of knowledge and subjecthood—not always on the "politically correct" side of struggles over rights and entitlements emerging from the popular classes and social sectors (sometimes in response to their own teachings), as the role of Luther in the German Peasant Revolts illustrates. In post-Tridentine Spain, in particular, the humanists in both secular and clerical forms had become, in effect, the organic intellectuals of Hapsburg absolutism, constituting the dominant critical-academic establishment and the functionaries of the elaborate and sophisticated censorship system erected by the Spanish Inquisition. This is not just a case of the co-optation of a potentially progressive intelligentsia and the new secular literary forms it championed by the Counter-Reformation and the aristocratic courts of the Baroque, as happened in seventeenth-century Italian culture. The ideological ambivalence of the humanities and literature was part of their conditions of origin and being in early modern Europe, particularly in those areas of the Hapsburg empire (Spain, Portugal and southern Italy, Latin America, the periphery of what would become the Austro-Hungarian Empire) where, because of the force of the Counter-Reformation, the transition to a bourgeois-democratic culture, marked by an increasing separation of church and state, was retarded.

In this context, literature and literary connoisseurship became sites of cultural representation in which the conflict between value systems of the aristocracy and the emerging bourgeoisie and plebeian sectors—a conflict that in places like Spain must have seemed like the nature of things itself rather than a historical phase—could be both expressed and mediated, in a fashion similar to the one Viswanathan suggests for the role of English literature in colonial India. The humanists themselves, with their foundation in the revival of classical rhetoric, were always aware that the purpose of their pedagogy was to produce the subject form of a ruling class (or classes). The specific character of that class—

merchant, feudal, bourgeois, absolutist dynasty, sect—was less important to them. In Golden Age Spain and its colonial empire, the "other" of the *letrado* was the *vulgo*—the masses—even that part of them that might be functionally literate but lacked the sort of training in humanities and general culture necessary to understand highly elaborated texts like Garcilaso's sonnet. As Anthony Grafton and Lisa Jardine note, the literature-based program of studies in the Renaissance academies

> fitted the needs of the new Europe that was taking shape, with its closed governing élites, hereditary offices and strenuous efforts to close off debate on vital political and social questions. It stamped the more prominent members of the new élite with an indelible cultural seal of superiority, it equipped lesser members with fluency and the learned habit of attention to textual detail and it offered everyone a model of true culture as something given, absolute, to be mastered, not questioned—and thus fostered in all its initiates a properly docile attitude towards authority. . . . In the Renaissance as in other periods, in sum, the price of collaboration in the renewal of art and literature was collaboration in the construction of society and polity.[7]

Let me now turn to a consideration of Garcilaso's sonnet itself. (Since one of the main genres of humanism was and is the literary essay, based on "close" textual reading and commentary, I am aware that in producing this reading I am also enacting a humanist ideology of the literary, as you are in reading it.) Here is the text as it appears in most current editions of Garcilaso's poetry (there is a variant of line 4), with both spelling and punctuation modernized, followed by my own prose gloss in English:

> En tanto que de rosa y azucena
> se muestra la color en vuestro gesto,
> y que vuestro mirar ardiente, honesto,
> enciende al corazón y lo refrena;
>
> y en tanto que el cabello, que en la vena
> del oro se escogió, con vuelo presto,
> por el hermoso cuello blanco, enhiesto,
> el viento mueve, esparce y desordena;

coged de vuestra alegre primavera
el dulce fruto, antes que el tiempo airado
cubra de nieve la hermosa cumbre.

Marchitará la rosa el viento helado,
todo lo mudará la edad ligera,
por no hacer mudanza en su costumbre.

[While the colors of the rose and the lily / show on your face / and your gaze, ardent and chaste, / ignites the heart and restrains it; // and while your hair, / touched in the vein of gold, with quick flight / against your stiff, white neck / the breeze moves, scatters, and disorders; // seize from your happy springtime / the sweet fruit, before haughty time / covers the handsome mountaintop with snow. // Icy wind will wither the rose, / light-footed age will transform everything / in order not to transform itself.]

Like most sonnets in the Romance languages, sonnet 23 is a Petrarchan sonnet made up of two quartets and two tercets, with an ABBA ABBA CDE DCE rhyme scheme. Thematically, it represents a variation on the carpe diem topos of Latin Silver Age poetry, mediated intertextually through a number of previous Italian Renaissance sonnets and *canzone* on the theme that must have served Garcilaso as models of imitation. Syntactically, it is composed of a long sentence lasting the first eleven lines, and a second shorter one—forming a sort of coda—in the second tercet.

As Jakobson and Lévi-Strauss noted in their essay on Baudelaire's "Les Chats," the tendency of the Petrarchan sonnet is for the implicit octet formed by the initial quartets to oppose the sestet formed by the two tercets. In sonnet 23 this possibility is articulated as follows: the octet is a conditional clause established by the "en tanto" (while) that introduces both quartets. In this synchronic verbal-visual space a portrait of the mistress of the (implicitly male?) speaking subject is drawn by means of an allegorized representation of four physical features of her head: her skin, eyes, hair, and neck.

By virtue of both the contradictions within, or between, these four features and the strain caused by the abnormally extended conditional clause, there is an accumulating tension within the synchrony of the octet, a tension suggested in the final line by the movement of the hair, which the breeze "mueve, esparce y desordena" (moves, scatters, and disorders). This tension is resolved and released by the articulation of the active verb, the imperative "coged," in the hinge between the octet and the sestet, followed closely by the direct object, "el dulce fruto" (the sweet fruit).

Thus the nuclear form of the sentence that occupies the octet and the first tercet is "you gather the fruit"; in other words, carpe diem. There are verb constructions in the octet such as "mueve, esparce y desordena," but they are subsumed and contained within the overarching stasis of the "en tanto." "Coged" opens up the flow of time (and the normal flow of the sentence) repressed or inhibited in the octet, setting up a syntactic-semantic isomorphism with the sonnet's opposition of sexual arousal and denial at the thematic level.

The sestet is then diachrony: flux, sexual enjoyment or *jouissance*, history (the biological historicity of the individual or of the species). These connotations are made explicit in the mobilization by allusion of the allegorical scheme of the ages of man/ages of metal/seasons of the year, in which youth equals springtime ("vuestra alegre primavera") equals the Golden Age, and old age equals winter ("cubra de nieve la hermosa cumbre") equals the Age of Iron. This antagonism between inhibition and flow in the syntactic and thematic structure of the sonnet is replicated at the level of its semantic field. All the semantic elements in the poem are organized by the polarity of "rosa" and "azucena," rose and lily, in the first line, there describing the contrast of the woman's white complexion with the red blush of her cheeks. It goes without saying that the red or "rosa" axis is associated with erotic gratification, the white or "azucena" axis with chastity and sexual renunciation. Thus, along the "rosa" axis are "ardiente" (burning), "enciende" (lights), the "vena de oro" (vein of gold) of the hair, its "vuelo presto" ("presto" is a neologism, which means, as in music, light and quick), and the "alegre primavera" (happy springtime) and "dulce fruto" (which suggests the apple of the Garden of Eden) of the sestet. Along the "azucena" axis are "honesto," "refrena" (restrains), the white skin and musculature of the neck, which is "enhiesto"—stiff, or rigid like marble—and thus finally the "nieve" of the sestet—the snow of winter, the white hair of old age.

Between the two systems there are a number of what the Mannerists would have called *contraposti*, or conceited oppositions. Thus, for example, the "mirar" (eyes, gaze) is "ardiente" and "honesto" at the same time, and as such both ignites like fire ("enciende") and inhibits like something cold ("refrena") the speaker's desire. The opposition between the hair (movement) and the neck (rigidity) in the second quartet is emphasized by the partial identity of the rhyme words relating to each: "presto"/"enhiesto."

The short sentence of the final tercet recapitulates the previous system of contradiction and mediation. "Marchitará" suggests not so much the idea of shriveling as a loss of intensity of color, something red becoming white or bleached out. The "viento" or breeze that disordered the hair in the slow motion of the octet becomes here the sterner, wintry "viento helado" of a movement of time that will transform everything in its path so as not to change its own nature ("por no hacer mudanza en su costumbre"). "Mudanza"/ "costumbre" form a final opposition, echoing the initial one of "rosa"/"azucena," with "costumbre" designating routine and immobility and "mudanza" growth and change (but also decay).

As we have come to expect in densely constructed verbal objects of this sort, an indeterminacy of meaning arises between the explicit message of the poem and the rhetorical machinery put in motion to present it. The message is something like the following: the woman's attractiveness as a sexual object is defined by the tension between her erotic and her sublimated sides manifest in her portrait. But if she allows the "azucena" side to dominate, that will lead to an unfulfilled old age in which her beauty will be lost: "cubra de nieve la hermosa cumbre." On the other hand, the move from virginity or preservation of virtue to erotic release and enjoyment—which itself follows a suggestion that the system of the octet is becoming excessive, "desordenado"—introduces the realm of time, "mudanza," and this necessarily also brings in its wake the reality of aging and decay. So actually having sex seems not to be the point either (this is a curiously unerotic erotic poem). The point is rather the poem itself and the new sort of literary connoisseurship it gives rise to.

As an abstraction from direct experience, from the presence of the lover and the sexual desire it engenders, sonnet 23 is itself part of the "white" or "azucena" axis. The poem, in effect, constructs its own ideology, based on an eminently nominalist sense that this is not just a question of an abstract idea or doctrine of the literary (or for that matter of sexual hedonism), but rather of the articulation of literature itself as a new form of human practice and experience. As an object of (a new kind of) desire, however, sonnet 23 belongs with the rose axis.[8]

But these dynamics also involve the articulation of a historicism. The age of a perpetual present of sinless erotic gratification is the Golden Age, "la alegre primavera." This is the time before history, moral law, and the state, before writing—the time of *otium*, of a pastoral Arcadia. But this is also a time of perpetual infancy. History introduces the possibility of achievement and transformation, ripening and maturation, just as the linguistic work of composition of the poem sublimates and eternalizes its subject. This can lead, as in epic or religious narrative, to the possibility of cultural apotheosis, but also to a loss of quality and a degradation, as in the ages of the lesser metals.

If we understand rose and lily as denoting the poles of an ideological struggle internal to the poem (as in—if the anachronism may be permitted—"Reds" and "Whites" as the two classes or class blocs in conflict in the Russian Revolution), then in a historical context defined in Western Europe by the transition from feudalism to capitalism, the rose (read as the affirmation of this-worldly sensual pleasure, the authority of experience over doctrine, empiricism, and the pleasures and indeterminacy of literature itself as against religious moralism) represents the values of a bourgeoisie in formation, while, as in the Russian Revolution, the lily represents the aristocracy and its religious ideological superstructure (as the flower associated with Christ and the Virgin Birth).

But the system of opposition in the poem is not just between the rose and the lily, but also between the stasis represented by the octet and the diachrony represented by the sestet. Within the stasis/flux opposition, the rose axis is also partly involved in the denial or suspension of the possibility of historical change, since its intention is to idealize the present: it is articulating an ideology of the lyrical. If the historicism of bourgeois revolution requires, as in the case of the Puritans, the legitimization of a *new* stage of history—the idea of progress or reconciliation with destiny—then the rose axis of sonnet 23 is, in a sense, the more reactionary side, and the denial of erotic gratification represented by the lily the more progressive, because the attendant requirement of sublimation has the potential of displacing eroticism toward ethical and utilitarian priorities. Courtly love—with its idealization of the woman as object of pleasure—is, after all, an ideology and a practice of aristocratic behavior, whereas the Reformation articulation of sexuality and sensual pleasure tended, as we know, to puritanism and misogyny.[9] So there is finally no clear correspondence between the polarities rose/lily and bourgeoisie/aristocracy, although traces of the contradiction between these two classes and at least partial aspects of their ideological superstructures are active in the symbolic and formal system of sonnet. What is worth remarking additionally is the way the subject-object allegory in the sonnet is gender-inflected. The one with the power of representation (of literature, of organizing that which is without significance in itself) is the implicitly male speaking voice; the (necessarily mute?) object *of* representation is the woman. In early modern Europe, both the graphic and literary images of America are of a nude or seminude woman with feathers in her hair, riding a crocodile)[10] so that figuration of the role of the male as sexual "initiator" in the Petrarchan love poem may be implicitly written over the relation between "man" and colonial space, and elites and subaltern subjects (which are gendered as feminine). The woman represented in sonnet 23 seems to have in her reluctance to submit to the desire of the speaking subject a power *over* the man, coincident with the overvalorization of the feminine in the discourse of courtly love;

but it is a power (and then one no longer of life and death) that the sonnet itself circumscribes and then subordinates to its own logic.

Let me summarize where I think we have arrived with this: around a phallogocentric figuration of the woman as the object of male desire, in Garcilaso's sonnet 23 the literary text in its most intimate formal and linguistic mechanisms has been converted into a space of ideological negotiation between the conceptions of history and the corresponding value worlds of a still-dominant feudal and a newly emerging bourgeois order. This negotiation is itself founded on a formalist ideology of the literary that derives from the humanist concern with eloquence, good writing, and literary connoisseurship—a concern that, in turn, founds the practice not only of the writer but also of the reader and critic. As in the contingent case of the Renaissance pastoral, such a procedure works to affirm hegemony not by its coincidence with the official representation of power, morality, and authority but precisely by its difference from it. The poem sets up a sphere of private experience and private self that is distinct from but not in contradiction with the public sphere and public identity of the subject as a social agent.

Would it be fair to say that what we are accustomed to calling literature and dealing with as such in our work is the history of this negotiation? If so, there is something not only historically determined but also neurotic and compulsive about literature—a way that even in its most contemporary and avant-garde forms it continues to replay endlessly the trauma of its moment of origin in a period of, as Marx's English translators felicitously named it, "the primitive accumulation of capital." What we can sense in the aporias of sonnet 23 is something like the *unconscious* of the literary, an unconscious that is present in its effects in any subsequent act of literary creation, however different the personal, historical, and cultural circumstances in which it takes place. To transpose Paul de Man's remark that the resistance to theory is theory itself, the ideology of the literary is literature itself.

I will outline in more detail some of the implications of this in the chapter that follows on the Spanish literary Baroque.

What I would like to offer in the second part of this chapter, however, is a note on the relation of contemporary humanistic practice to the issues involved in what I am calling the ideology of the literary. I propose to do this through a consideration of Stephen Greenblatt's book, *Marvelous Possessions: The Wonder of the New World*, published in anticipation of the Columbian quincentenary.[11] I have chosen *Marvelous Possessions*, which is about the discourse of travel in fifteenth- and sixteenth-century Europe, for two reasons: (1) it is an ambitious attempt to apply the procedures of the new historicism to the question of the representation of the New World in the years immediately preceding and following 1492, and as such is an exemplary text of contemporary academic humanism; (2) Greenblatt is centrally concerned in it with the recognition of the involvement of literature and humanistic culture in the process of conquest and colonization of the New World.

I will argue that while the intention of *Marvelous Possessions* (and of Greenblatt's work generally) is clearly to contribute to a dismantling of the structures of colonial, Eurocentric discourse in the humanities, there are still some assumptions of this discourse operative in its own intellectual protocols. These assumptions have to do, in particular, with its perpetuation at one level of the ideology of the literary we have identified in the Garcilaso sonnet, which at another level it puts into question.

Marvelous Possessions is divided into four chapters, which concern, respectively: (1) *Mandeville's Travels*, a popular book of imaginary voyages that predates 1492 and offers, Greenblatt thinks, a possible, but ultimately neglected, paradigm of a "tolerant possession" of the non-European other; (2) the representation of the New World in what Greenblatt calls "the founding speech act" (65) of Columbus's diary and letters on his first voyage; (3) the question of understanding and misunderstanding Indian speech and sign languages in a series of different narratives of exploration and conquest; and (4) the role of testimonial witnessing and of translation and translators in the negotiation of representation of the New World. This final chapter, titled "The Go-Between," culminates in a celebration of, on the one hand, Hernán

Cortés's Indian translator and mistress, Doña Marina, and, on the other, of Montaigne as cultural agents of a "critical and humanizing power of the marvelous" that can be counterposed to the instrumental use of the marvelous in the colonial discourse of conquest and possession. The design of the book is thus cyclical (and, as we will see, self-reflective), moving from the playful unfixity of Mandeville's evocation of the marvelous in his imaginary travels, through its mobilization as "a redemptive, aestheticizing supplement to a deeply flawed legal ritual of appropriation" in Columbus and the conquistadores after 1492, to, in Montaigne's liberal skepticism—clearly a figure for Greenblatt's own—a "marvelous dispossession, a loss of the fiercely intolerant certainty that liscensed unbearable cruelty" (150).

Greenblatt begins his account with a striking act of aesthetic-ideological defamiliarization. He is, he tells us, going to be concerned with *petites histoires*, not *grands récits*, for "the discourse of travel in the late Middle Ages and the Renaissance is rarely if ever interesting at the level of sustained narrative and teleological design, but gripping at the level of the anecdote" (2). What such discourses show us is that

the Europeans who ventured to the New World in the first decades after Columbus's discovery shared a complex, well-developed, and, above all, mobile technology of power: writing, navigational instruments, ships, warhorses, attack dogs, effective armor, and highly lethal weapons. Their culture was characterized by an immense confidence in its own centrality, by a political organization based on practices of command and submission, by a willingness to use coercive violence on both strangers and fellow countrymen, and by a religious ideology centered on the endlessly proliferated representation of a tortured and murdered god of love. The cult of this male god—a deity whose earthly form was born from the womb of a virgin and sacrificed by his heavenly father to atone for human disobedience—in turn centered on a ritual . . . in which the god's flesh and blood were symbolically eaten. Such was the confidence of this culture that it expected perfect strangers—the Arawaks of the Caribbean, for example—to abandon their own beliefs, preferably immediately, and embrace those of Europe as luminously and self-evidently true. A failure to do so provoked impatience, contempt and even murderous rage. (9)

In the inclusion of writing in the list of technologies of power, Greenblatt means to allude to Todorov's account in *The Conquest of America*[12] of the centrality of the European practice of writing in the conquest as a "representational technology" superior to those of the indigenous civilizations. Because, in Todorov's view, the latter were oral and thus necessarily based on a ritualized repetition and memorization of formulas, unlike writing (which is "mobile"), they were marked by an inability to improvise and adapt to changing situations. But it is not so much as technology that writing and the culture of the book functioned, Greenblatt cautions—I think correctly—but rather as an ideology of the enterprise of conquest, an ideology based as all ideologies are on a misrecognition of the nature and limitations of the representational systems developed by the indigenous civilizations, a misrecognition that Todorov, with his privileging of a Eurocentric concept of *écriture*, seems to share.

The confrontation with that which is wholly unexpected, even undreamed, marvelous—say Columbus's first contact with the inhabitants of the islands he sighted, or Bernal Díaz's first vision of the Aztec capital—produces in the early European discourse of the New World, Greenblatt argues, a crisis of meaning, a rift or "cracking apart of contextual understanding in an elusive and ambiguous experience of wonder" (p. 19). This crisis relates the experience of discovery and conquest and its literary transcription to a larger series of inquiries in Renaissance aesthetics, theology, and philosophy dealing with the experience of the marvelous. "The marvelous is a central feature," Greenblatt observes, "in the whole complex system of representation, verbal and visual, philosophical and aesthetic, intellectual and emotional, through which people in the late Middle Ages and the Renaissance apprehended, and thence possessed or discarded, the unfamiliar, the alien, the terrible, the desirable, and the hateful" (22–23).

This problem of the assimilation of the other is, he adds, "linked to what we may call, adapting Marx, *the reproduction and circulation of mimetic capital*" (6). The last phrase is in italics in the original, and signals what in fact is the underlying trope of *Marvelous Possessions*, that of circulation, or, in the poststructuralist idiom Greenblatt sometimes prefers, of the inevitable errancy or unfixity of language and representation. The mention of Marx historicizes the trope, suggesting the linkage of mimetic (or cultural) capital to colonialism and capitalism in the formation of a world market in the sixteenth century.

Again and again in *Marvelous Possessions*, the image of circulation will be invoked as a signifier of both the European experience of the alterity of the New World and Greenblatt's own critical practice in the book. Thus, for example, Mandeville (whose own identity as a subject is a matter of dispute) offers

> a renunciation of possession, the critical pathway in a circulation of plagiarized, unstable signifiers through which a crusading drive toward the sacred rocks at the center of the world [the reference is to Jerusalem] is transformed into a tolerant perambulation along its rim. (24)

Or:

> The body of John Mandeville is a set of pieces that are set in motion, carried from one place to another, endlessly exchanged. . . . There is no original, no authorizing self, no authentic text. (48)

Or this on Montaigne's essay on cannibals:

> Montaigne conjures up a world that is always rolling, turning, slipping away, a world of perennial, inescapable circulation. (150)

But the most striking images of circulation come in Greenblatt's own insertion into the text through a series of what he calls "traveler's anecdotes (that are bound up with those I study" (3). One of these is a coda to the last chapter, where Greenblatt identifies himself, in the process of articulation that the book represents, with the role of the translator or "go-between" he has been discussing. In a village church in the valley of Oaxaca with "a charming painted interior with interesting wooden effigies, carved by local Indian sculptors instructed by the friars who had converted them," Greenblatt peers into a niche that features a recumbent figure of Jesus.

There, fixed in the plaster of the ceiling, out of view from the nave, was a stone carving of the Mixtec god of death. The image looked down directly at the face of the crucified god. These divinities have exchanged this sightless gaze, this perpetual circulation, for more than four hundred years. (150–51)

Framing the book from the other side, the introduction features a long account of some days spent in Bali. Here is part of it:

In August, 1986, on a tourist's typical first night in Bali, I walked by moonlight on narrow paths through silent rice paddies glittering with fireflies. I reached a tiny village which in the darkness I identified less by the low, half-hidden huts and temples than by the frenzied barking of the dogs at my approach. I saw a light from the *bale banjar*, the communal pavilion in which I knew—from having read Clifford Geertz and Miguel Covarrubias and Gregory Bateson and Margaret Mead—that the Balinese gathered in the evenings. I drew near and discovered that the light came from a television set that the villagers, squatting or sitting cross-legged, were intent on watching. Conquering my disappointment, I accepted the gestured invitation to climb on the platform and see the show: on the communal VCR, they were watching an elaborate temple ceremony. Alerted by the excited comments and whoops of laughter, I recognized in the genial crowd of television watchers on the platform several of the ecstatic celebrants, dancing in trance states, whom I was seeing on the screen.

We may call what I witnessed that evening the assimilation of the other. (3)

Perhaps to head off an anticipated criticism here, a footnote directs us to the following caveat:

Obviously we are not very far here from the politics and economics of world domination . . . but there is a kind of sentimental pessimism that simply collapses everything into a global vision of domination and subjection. To recognize and admire local accommodations is not uncritically to endorse capitalist markets. (152 n. 4)

One cannot but agree wholeheartedly with this observation, which has been central in the development of third world cultural studies; but it clearly misses the point. The problem

Greenblatt anticipates is not with what he calls the "imaginative adaptations" of poor people to conditions beyond their making or control that the anecdote reveals. It is with the quality of *his* perception of what is going on in both of these anecdotes. This perception betokens the experience of what I will call—in the spirit of Greenblatt's own concern with the marvelous—a postmodernist tourist sublime (of the same order as the pseudofeminist third world sublime Gayatri Spivak rather spectacularly denounced in Kristeva's *About Chinese Women*).[13]

For it is in these figurations of the relation of his own self to the synchronic and diachronic aporia of "the politics and economics of world domination" that Greenblatt's critical method and his ideological claims for new historicism as an oppositional practice come into a kind of correspondence. As Donald Pease noted apropos Greenblatt's earlier essay on *The Tempest* and colonialism:

> Greenblatt's new historicism activates a series of interlinked homologies holding together, in the transfer of their metaphors, colonial subjection, Renaissance subjects, theatricalized society, and academic discipline formation. The basis for these linkages inheres in a similarity between the way knowledge is ordinarily produced in an academic discipline (through a generalized structure of domination and subjection), the way native peoples are subjected to the generalized control of colonists, and the way actors submit to a script. Having joined together these otherwise unrelated realms, through the transits of his metaphors, Greenblatt defines the new historicism as different. Unlike colonialism or other academic disciplines or Renaissance culture, but like the ruler of a theater state, the new historicist, Greenblatt would claim, does not subject his practitioner to dominative structure but instead enables him to practice the evasion of all these interlinked homologies.[14]

Jameson makes a similar point in his critique of Walter Benn Michaels in his book on postmodernism. The stated concern with power and representation in Michaels and the new historicism generally, he suggests, may be in the nature of what the formalists called "a 'motivation of the device,' an entity invoked after the fact to rationalize the practice of collage or montage of multiple materials" that the school specializes in.[15] This suggests that the underlying assumption of the new historicism is in fact aestheticism: a "shared writing practice," in Jameson's words (184). Here is Greenblatt himself, in a passage from *Marvelous Possessions* that is strikingly reminiscent of Victor Shlovsky's definition of *ostranenie* or defamiliarization in "Art as Technique":

> This is the utopian moment of travel: when you realize that what seems most unattainably marvelous, most desirable, is what you already have, what you could have—if you could only strip away the banality and corruption of the everyday— at home. (25)

Greenblatt is acutely aware that the position of the university intellectual as the site for registering or ideologizing circulation is not a disinterested one, nor is it disconnected from the machinery of global domination. He claims no safe "aesthetic" distance from the Europeans he writes about:

> On the contrary, I have tried in these chapters, not without pain, to register within the very texture of my scholarship a critique of the Zionism in which I was raised and to which I continue to feel, in the midst of deep moral and political reservations, a complex bond. (ix)

I understand and sympathize with the nature of this predicament. But is not this indecision between the critique of Zionism and its affirmation as a response to the contingencies of Jewish history yet another version of "circulation," expressive of a wish to remain in the position of mediator or transcoder? It is symptomatic in this respect that Greenblatt chooses to leave this tension between critique and identification intact, thus providing the ground for the oscillation of subject position that *Marvelous Possessions* as an exercise represents, rather than attempting, as many Israelis have, to construct a decolonized or anticolonial version of Zionism. He would reply perhaps that that is outside the area of his competence or responsibility as a literary critic and teacher.

But in some situations one needs to take sides. What does it mean to take sides in today's world? It means, among other things, to enter into relations of solidarity, solidarity networks, and to orient one's work within the university or the education system in relation to this fact. But how does one choose with whom to side? With Edward Said's right to reclaim his childhood home in Jerusalem or the right of Jewish people to a refuge from oppression and genocide? With the Mixtec god of death or the Christian Jesus? Perhaps there is still a place—democratic socialism?—from which the antagonisms represented by these dichotomies can be sublated in the opposition of humanity to global exploitation and oppression. But to create that place is not the intention of *Marvelous Possessions*, which is itself fashioned as a literary artifact on the collapse of "great narratives" of emancipation. Unfortunately, as Greenblatt's "traveler's anecdotes" show, remaining in the nonteleological, aestheticized position of the "go-between" is also a way of choosing, choosing in this case the implication of the new historicism in postfordism and in the production of a corresponding postmodernist sublime, which will adjust humanistic culture and the humanities to the new patterns and practices of transnational capitalism.[16]

What the consequences of this impasse, which in one way or another we share with Greenblatt, are for our own work as teachers and critics of literature is by no means clear. As Viswanathan observes, "There are no simple lessons to be derived from this history, least of all the lesson that imperialism can be swiftly undone merely by hurling away the texts it institutionalized" (169). I share with her, though, the sense that when we teach literature today we also teach its implication in the construction of the world as it is. This involves understanding and accepting the fact that literature itself has to change in the course of mobilization for fundamental social change in any existing society, and particularly in postcolonial processes of cultural disalienation and appropriation, that these will necessarily involve a transformation of its dominant forms and a breakdown, or at least a renegotiation, of the distinctions on which its status and prestige have rested.

CHAPTER 3

On the Spanish Literary Baroque

Wit *is the capacity to exercise dictatorship.*

Walter Benjamin[1]

Like one of its major figures, Janus—"el bifronte dios" in Góngora's exact characterization (one face peering perhaps at the sunset of feudalism, the other at the dawn of capitalism)—the Baroque has been an ambivalent phenomenon; equally, its reception. The debate over its nature and value has been perennially on the agenda of modern European literary and cultural criticism, indeed was, in a sense, the issue that founded this criticism as such. What is at stake here is not only the Baroque as a "style-concept," but also its articulation as a cultural signifier, with a correspondingly variable set of signifieds, in the long history of ideological class conflict that accompanies the transition between feudalism and capitalism in Europe and the establishment of its colonial systems.

It is reductionist to argue, like Werner Weisbach,[2] that the Baroque was the art form of the Counter-Reformation (among other reasons because there was a Protestant Baroque), but perhaps not *too much* so. The pejorative connotation the term acquired in European art history comes from the Enlightenment attack (Boileau, Luzán) on the Baroque as a decadent and irrational style: in the case of Spain and Latin America, the aesthetic correlative, as it were, of the Black Legend. Hispanism as an academic field itself emerged in the context of the eighteenth-century debate over the *comedia*—the Baroque style of national theater developed by Lope de Vega in the seventeenth century—between the par-   47 tisans of Neoclassical poetics, who argued that the Spanish theater had to be modernized in accord with Enlightenment standards of rational good taste, and Catholic traditionalists, who defended the *comedia* as the expression of a Hispano-Catholic national genius in what amounted to a sort of literary feudal populism. This debate, via a dialectically tortuous route through Sturm und Drang, Herder, the French Revolution and the principle of the right of national liberation, Napoleon and the nationalist anti-Napoleonic guerrillas, and the aesthetics of Hegel and Kant, leads to Romanticism and in particular to the Schlegel brothers' concept of Romantic Art, exemplified for them above all by the Baroque drama of Calderón.

But if the Romantics resurrected some figures associated with the Baroque like Calderón or Bach, they did not revise the negative concept of the epoch as such. For an emerging and still-combated liberalism on the Hapsburg-Latin periphery of Europe, the Baroque was still seen at the end of the nineteenth century as an essentially reactionary cultural style (by, for example, Galdós and Antonio Machado in Spain, and Croce and Gramsci in Italy). Consequently, its revalorization, initiated by Heinrich Wölfflin's *Principles of Art History*, would be contingent on the crisis of liberalism that accompanied World War I and the Russian Revolution (*Principles* was more or less contemporary with Lenin's *Imperialism*, Lukács's *Theory of the Novel*, and Spengler's *Decline of the West*). In turn, the emerging ideology of aesthetic Modernism in its fascist or corporatist (Eugenio D'Ors, Spengler, Pound, Eliot), liberal (Ortega and the Spanish Generation of '27), and Marxist (Benjamin) variants would recuperate the Baroque—and invert the Romantic hierarchy of symbol over allegory—in its own "invention of tradition," to borrow Eric Hobsbawm's phrase.

One point of contact with Modernism was that the Baroque is by antonomasia a "difficult" style. The Italian Mannerists in the sixteenth century had advanced the idea of difficulty as such—*difficoltà*—as an aesthetic property. They held that a special pleasure was to be gained through the ability of mind (*acutezza*) to experience the artwork as an intricate space of signification. The point was related to a Neoplatonic argument in favor of artistic intuition and freedom that amounted to a kind of protoformalism. What counted for the Mannerists was the subtle logic of the *dispositio*, not the *materia*. By contrast, the leitmotif of Góngora's *detractores* in the seventeenth century—post-Tridentine humanists like Francisco de Cascales, who claimed to represent an Aristotelian "discipline of the rules" in literature—was that the cultivation of difficulty for its own sake betrayed a contradiction of the Scholastic entailment of *res* and *verba*, of language and that which language represents. By seeming to posit conceptual wit (*ingenio*) as the primary basis for aesthetic pleasure, they felt, Góngora and his followers produced a discourse that was nugatory and functionally atheistic.

The element of difficulty and excess in Baroque writing in particular links to the question of who read in Golden Age Spain and its colonies anyway. Early modern texts are ubiquitously disfigured by the sort of linguistic modernization favored by formalist philologists (suppression of capitalization of some nouns, and capital letters at the start of lines of verse, changes in punctuation, paragraphing, and spelling, etc.).[3] In like fashion, there is a natural tendency to misrecognize their nature and function as cultural artifacts by considering them as if they were in their initial moment of production and circulation the same thing they are when we encounter them today as part of an academically constructed and sanctioned canon of "Spanish literature."

The notion of literature as something available to a reading public at large is historically linked in Europe to the commodification of literary production and distribution, and to the growth of mass public education, particularly in the nineteenth century. As the cases of both the Baroque *comedia* and *Don Quijote* suggest, such a commodification was well under way in seventeenth-century Spain. The book industry was one of the first forms of capitalist production and merchandising in Spain and Europe generally. In one of his last adventures, Don Quijote visits a factory in Barcelona—then as now the most highly developed capitalist enclave on the Iberian peninsula—where books like *Don Quijote* are composed, printed, and bound. That, for all practical purposes, is the end of Don Quijote, both the hero and the novel. It is not until the period of ascendant liberalism on the heels of the French Revolution in the late eighteenth and early nineteenth centuries, however, that the virtual monopoly of the church and the aristocracy on higher education and literacy (of the sort required for the "appreciation" of complex literary works) is decisively broken, and that something like a large, socially diverse reading public begins to emerge in Europe.

By contrast, we know that certain forms of Baroque literature were in fact designed to resist even the already-existing possibilities of commercial publication and distribution in seventeenth-century Spain, since their instrumentality was not at all to "reach" a mass audience but rather to intervene in discrete circuits of aristocratic power and patronage. The mode of existence of literature and literary texts in precapitalist societies—even in a transitional, late-feudal (or, if you prefer, early modern) one like Golden Age Spain, already marked by a flourishing book trade—was in several respects quite different than it is in our own, something that should lead us to regard with suspicion the notion of literature itself as an unchanging essence.

To begin with, there is the fact that some eighty percent of the population could neither read nor write (and that this was regarded as a *normal* state of things, as compared to our contemporary anxiety about illiteracy).[4] This did not mean that this section of the public was necessarily barred from literature altogether. Wlad Godzich and Nicholas Spadaccini have drawn attention to the emergence in the sixteenth century of a mass-oriented "auditive culture"—the concept comes from the Brazilian critic Luiz Costa Lima—that differed from both traditional oral poetry and narrative, dependent on recitation from memory, and the written/published text produced for the private consumption, through the market mechanism or not, of a reader or readers. Such a culture might involve, for example, the *comedia*, which could engage its audience in extremely complicated word play, or the common practice of reading books aloud to audiences described several times in the *Quijote*, or what is called *poesía de cordel*, literally "poems on a string" (because they were sold at market this way)—texts that could be orally delivered but were composed in written form and published cheaply in some form or other (one of the earliest forms of the Top 40 hit is the *pliego suelto* or printed song sheet, which survives in the Mexican *corridos* or narrative ballads). Such discursive forms are characterized in Godzich and Spadaccini's words "by a high level of rhetorical fabrication" dependent on the new possibilities of expression developed in Renaissance vernacular literature. "Although orally delivered, [they do] not seek to establish a dialogical relation with the audience but instead to leave the audience dumbfounded: *boca abierta.*" The Baroque penchant for difficulty, which is supposed to be a mark of its differentiation from the illiterate or semiliterate *vulgo*, produces paradoxically a popular taste for extravagant syntax and images.[5]

The most influential theorist and one of the most important practitioners of Baroque *écriture* in Spain was the Jesuit Baltasar Gracián. Anyone who has read Gracián will be familiar with the extreme artificiality of his writing. This involves not only its elliptical *conceptista* syntax and its very dense play of intertextual allusion, but also its extremely intricate structural design, which is masked by its aphoristic surface form. What is curious is how such an intensely and explicitly literary writing could in any sense be seen as effective, as Gracián certainly intended it to be, as a "mirror of princes" or guide to statecraft in the fashion of Machiavelli—particularly in a situation of imperial *descenso* or decline, where new forms of political imagination and practice were urgently needed. In fact, it was *not* effective in this sense; it was a symptom of decadence rather than renewal. But I am more interested here in exploring the nature of its claim to be effective.

In part, the claim had something to do with the discovery of the nonreferential, generative properties of language by what Noam Chomsky has called Cartesian linguistics— surely one of the most important epistemological foundations of Baroque culture generally.[6] In part too, however, the claim fits with what we know about the nature of aristocratic dictatorship itself as a power system. In José Antonio Maravall's well-known thesis,[7] the Spanish Baroque represents a "lyrical engineering of the human world" by the absolutist state. This is not a case of cultural activity directing itself to a power center from the outside, in the way both mass and elite cultures are related to the state in contemporary liberal societies. In the Spanish court and the colonial viceroyalties of the Golden Age, art and politics are not yet clearly separate disciplines and activities. That is why for Gracián an *arte de agudeza* based on the study of literary conceits—*conceptos*—could be seen as a prerequisite for the formation of the Baroque man of affairs, the *político*.

But this extreme dependence on cultural production for securing and developing rule also entailed what in contemporary philosophy would be termed an "antifoundationalist" conception of politics and power. This is implicit in Gracián's theory of the conceit itself, which, as A. A. Parker stressed, begins with the distinction between *agudeza de artificio*—literary wit, justified by aesthetic criteria—and *agudeza de perspicacia*—philosophical intelligence, the ability to see relations that are logically and objectively true. In his famous definition in his treatise on poetic language, *Agudeza y arte de ingenio*, of the *concepto* as "an act of the mind that expresses the correspondence found between things" ("un acto del entendimiento, que exprime la correspondencia que se halla entre los objetos") (discurso II), Gracián was not proposing a symbolist poetics of correspondence of hidden essences, but stressing precisely the arbitrary and formalistic character of linguistic signification. For, Gracián observed, "This correspondence is generic to all conceits, and embraces all the artifice of wit, for even though it be established by counterposition or dissonance, that too is an artful connection of objects" ("Esta correspondencia es genérica a todos los conceptos, y abraza todo el artificio del ingenio, que aunque éste sea por contraposición y disonancia, aquello mismo es artificiosa conexión de los objetos").[8]

What is continually deferred in Gracián is the resolution of the ambiguity between such a rhetorical notion of the discursive construction of power and meaning—what Nietzsche must have admired in his work—and the notion of power as an expression of an innate quality (*quilate rey*, or "carat" of the king, to use one of Gracián's own favorite expressions) demanded both by aristocratic caste assumptions and Counter-Reformation political-moral theory. Gracián sustains this deferral by substituting a logic of appearances for a logic of essences. As he notes in one of the central maxims of his essay *El Héroe*, "This first rule of greatness advises that, if not to be infinite, then to appear so, which is not an ordinary subtlety" ("Esta primera regla de grandeza aprende: si no el ser infinitos, aparcerlo, que no es sutileza común"). The means of this deferral is the practice of writing itself: literature.

Jean-Cristophe Agnew has argued that the development of Elizabethan and Jacobean theater in England coincided with the onset of market society in the context of the primitive accumulation of capital. Where the *marketplace* was a necessary but liminal institution in feudal society, the *market* came to seem as coextensive with (and determinant of) society itself. The expansion of exchange relations and the increasing importance of money disrupted traditional hierarchies of social status and privilege, producing what Agnew calls a "crisis of representation" that the emerging secular theater both reflected and deepened.

David Hildner has written of the tensions between idea and action in Calderón's characters as indicating an "increasing divorce between the ideological foundations of the Spanish empire (mainly Scholastic theology) and the actual course its rulers followed." The Thomist notion of authority rooted in a divinely ordained (and rational) order of things yields to a situation where "the prime requisite is *invención*, the art of finding (*invenire*) arguments and rhetorical devices to win practical battles." "In this connection it is interesting to study," Hildner adds, "how the doctrine of the divine right of kings had to be modified when it became evident that a *valido* like Olivares could be a better ruler than the king himself."[9]

Segismundo's final remark in *La vida es sueño*—"Why does this surprise you if my teacher was a dream?" ("¿qué os espanta si fue mi maestro un sueño?")—is a response to Basilio telling him how wise and prudent he appears to have become. In making it, he is letting it be known—discreetly, politically—that he accepts the pretense Basilio puts forward that his first disaster as a ruler was just a dream, instead of a charade organized by Basilio to test him. By not directly indicting Basilio, he shows—as in his rejection of Rosaura—a capacity for sublimation or *prudencia*. This would certainly be an instance of what Hildner means by "invención" in the behavior of the prince.

But there is a related reading. The last speech of a *comedia* conventionally announces the title and asks of the audience, like Segismundo, "perdón de nuestras faltas" (pardon for our faults). To do so, the speaker must simultaneously speak in character and step out of it to reveal himself or herself as an actor playing a role. This is what Segismundo does. The idea of "fue mi maestro un sueño" thus becomes a figure for the play—*La vida es sueño*—that has just been completed. What is dreamlike about Segismundo's new status and power is that it is based on a fiction. An aesthetics—Lope's *engañar con la verdad* (deceive with the truth) of well-made theatrical intrigue—has become here the epistemology of a new politics. In the Calderonian allegory of the "great theater of the world," Segismundo has become aware of the arbitrary, "semiotic" character of social authority and roles; on the other hand, he will also insist on the *necessity* of these remaining as they are.

Segismundo's problem in *La vida es sueño* is that he cannot square his sense—a Scholastic one—of his legitimacy and right to rule with the fact that he is empirically excluded from power. It is not only that Calderón is offering a model of this predicament in the play; the play itself enacts the solution of the problem, which is the practice of literature itself as the foundation for the subject form of the ruling class.

But this is not only a matter of the overvaluation of literature as such, the displacement of dogma or science by "invención"; there is also the question of the particular *kinds* of literature favored by the literary Baroque—its redefinition of the criteria of literary taste. This involves, roughly speaking, a shift from *materia*, as defined by the neo-Aristotelian articulation in Renaissance literary theory of established (narrative) genres, to *dispositio* or something like the poststructuralist idea of *écriture*: the cultivation of writing detached from referential or doctrinal function. This could involve, among other things, the transgression of previous principles of generic or stylistic decorum, or the taste for cathacresis, dissonance, or the bizarre (precisely because such things demonstrated a more intense aesthetic-conceptual *artificio*). Above all, the new aesthetics tends, however, as in Gracián's own *Agudeza y arte de ingenio*, to the "anthology" of individual acts of wit that can be isolated and studied as such.

One of the most famous *conceptos* of the Spanish literary Baroque is Góngora's description of Angelica's feet in his poem *Angélica y Medoro* (105–9), a reworking of the scene in Ariosto's *Orlando furioso* where Roland comes upon the glade where the two lovers are hidden and in a jealous rage destroys it (Angelica is the Chinese princess he has fallen in love with; Medoro a wounded Moorish warrior she nurses back to health):

> El pie calza en lazos de oro,
> porque la nieve se goce,
> y no se vaya por pies
> la hermosura del orbe

[She wears straps of gold (sandals) on her feet / so that the snow can delight in itself (by contrast) / and so that the beauty of this earth / should not run away on its feet (or run out by feet)]

Dámaso Alonso glossed this as follows, borrowing E. M. Wilson's note that the expression "irse por pies" meant to flee or run away in Golden Age Spanish: "I assumed that 'lazos de oro' has two aims: as 'gold' it was meant to set off the snowy whiteness of Angelica's skin, and as 'straps' to prevent 'the beauty of the world'—Angelica—from fleeing (one should recall the furtive and venturesome character Angelica is given in Ariosto)."[10]

This by no means exhausts the possibilities of meaning in the conceit. But what I want to stress are simply its extreme artificiality and excess, even by the very generous standards of Baroque discourse, in relation to its referent. It is precisely as such, however, that these lines condense most acutely the poem as a whole, which is itself a displacement of a previous narrative epic form, modeled on and directly or indirectly legitimizing the military *telos* of European colonialism, in favor of an aesthetic and erotic utopia of two non-European and non-Christian lovers constructed in the narrative ballad form of Castilian folk poetry, the *romance*, with its characteristic truncated or subjunctive ending.

What Gracián was arguing, in effect, is that such conceits were a new modality for the education of political power, which was now to be founded not in any "content" like the Christian humanism of Ariosto's epic, but simply on the exercise (*ejercicio*) demanded by the complexity of the linguistic elaboration itself.

Something like the conceit in *Angélica y Medoro* preserved the range and sublimity of epic as a form of class discourse, in a situation where the actual narration in interminable *octavas reales* of a military expedition or foundation was beginning to be felt to be not only anachronistic, out of fashion, but also potentially confusing or destabilizing, given the new realities of power politics faced by the Spanish monarchy and colonial viceroyalties in the seventeenth century. The imperial *descenso* demanded more the strategy of the fox than of the lion, Gracián's *discreto* or *político* (formed by the study of literary conceits) more than his *héroe* (formed by epic and moral *exempla*). It was the minor forms of poetry developed by Gongorism—"occasional" poems, *romances*, *villancicos, loas, letrillas satíricas*, and the like—that offered effective models of a new, post-epic and posthumanist literature in which the everyday activities of Spanish or colonial civil society could be represented and idealized. It was precisely by being minor that these forms assumed their centrality and importance in Baroque literary practice. As in the case of our own postmodernity, a series of prior "great narratives" and their generic forms (epic, pastoral, tragedy, etc.) no longer serve to either represent or legitimize effectively the existing or desired relations of power/knowledge. In their place appears the literary culture of sonnets, essays, allegories, fragments, *perlas, crisis*, miniatures, *primores* that Gracián both theorizes and anthologizes.

A number of Baroque literary texts—*Angélica y Medoro* is one—circulated only in hand-lettered manuscript copies among the literary circles—*tertulias*—of the court and the viceroyalties. Their readers are literally a "select" few: the court aristocracy—the *grandes*—and its retinue of chaplains, secretaries, advisers, clerks, and so on. (Góngora boasts that he writes "not for the many" ["no para los muchos"].) The organic intellectual of Hapsburg imperialism was, as I noted in the discussion of Garcilaso's sonnet 23, the *letrado*. To be a *letrado* signified two things: (1) to at least claim aristocratic and Old Christian lineage (*limpieza de sangre*); and (2) to be adept at one or another of the differentiated but interrelated intellectual disciplines that formed the basis of aristocratic hegemony. These disciplines—jurisprudence, theology, history, rhetoric, canon law, administration, humanities, *arbitrismo* (political economy), politics, and so on—have in common, despite their respective technical specificities, the need to be elaborated in or by a written discourse stylistically compatible with the religious-seigneurial supposition of an innate authority or right to rule. Baroque elite literature of the sort Gracián was theorizing aspires to fill this need, to provide a literary style for the self-representation and legitimization of state functionaries. What it transmits to the court is not only the sign of aristocratic elevation—*honor*— but also a technique of power, an exercise or formal simulacrum of the ability to understand, organize, control, and sublimate. That is why a well-wrought sonnet or *auto sacramental* could be a means for insertion and advancement in the court bureaucracy by a *hidalgo* of otherwise modest background.

What is implicit here is an argument of the following sort, common to both a Weberian and a Marxist analytic of state formation: there is a connection between the emergence of the social division of manual and intellectual labor and the emergence of the state as a special social institution. State forms and functions are products of a centralization and/or monopolization of certain types of intellectual labor, among them the exercise of literacy and the production and dissemination of written discourse. The resulting equation of knowledge and power underlies public ideology (in the sense of official state doctrine) and its role in legitimizing the state to its subjects, so that it appears to them as the bearer of an intrinsic providence or rationality. But there is also the question of those primary forms of ideology in which the state represents itself to itself, that uphold relations between its various members, units, and activities, that define the parameters of its potential self-consciousness.[11]

Clifford Geertz has written of the "theatre state" of seventeenth-century Bali as follows:

> The stupendous cremations, tooth filings, temple dedications, pilgrimages, and blood sacrifices, mobilizing hundreds and even thousands of people and great quantities of wealth, were not means to political ends: they were the ends themselves, they were what the state was for. Court ceremonialism was the driving force of court politics; and mass ritual was not a device to shore up the state, but rather the state, even in its final gasp, was a device for the enactment of mass ritual. . . . The ritual life of the court, and in fact the life of the court generally, is thus paradigmatic, not merely reflective, of social order.[12]

The image is intentionally formalistic (Geertz does not trouble to explain the forms of feudal extraction that provided, among other things, the revenues for such spectacles). But it does help us to understand the Baroque's sense of the autonomy and centrality of cultural practice.

The Baroque's major institutional and ideological form is the city, whose rise all over Europe as an international, national and/or regional corporate *seigneur* involved, as John Merrington has noted, "not only a massive shift of human and material resources in favor of urban concentrations, but also a *conquest* over the countryside, which becomes ruralized, since it by no means represented in the past an exclusively agricultural milieu."[13] As an essentially urban cultural form, the Baroque implies a taste for the new and the artificial, for example fireworks (*fuegos de artificio*), which, Maravall notes, "were an adequate sign of the splendor of whoever ordered them because of their very artifice, their difficulty, the expense in human labor and in money that they implied" (246).

But the taste for the artificial also carries with it for a Baroque sensibility the fear of moral or ecological perversion—the transgression of the Horatian golden mean—and a consequent nostalgia for "the simple life" represented in idealized form by the pastoral. Góngora features elaborate fireworks scenes throughout his poetry. In the *Soledades* (I, 642–58), there is a fireworks display above a village to celebrate the impending wedding of a peasant couple. An old man who witnesses the spectacle fears, however, that, on the analogy of Phaeton's chariot, an accident will happen "and miserably / the village that greeted the night / will make at dawn a sterile field" ("y miserablemente / campo amanezca estéril de ceniza / la que anocheció aldea").

This same cult of (and anxiety about) the artificial characterizes those elite forms of Baroque culture that are internal to the life of the court, such as Góngora's poems. These embody the aristocratic fetish of a highly wrought art form, which is seen as noble or sublime to the extent that it eludes the comprehension of the masses and situates itself outside the nascent bourgeois value system of money and market exchange as determinants of power and status. In Baroque representation, for example in the key symbol of the cornucopia, wealth and power appear as uncoerced reflexes of some providence built into nature itself, rather than as products of human labor carried out under exploitative and, in the case of the colonies, genocidal relations of production. This is part of its service as an ideological practice for and of a seigneurial, Catholic ruling class that needs to differentiate itself from the sordid world of commerce and manual labor at the same time that it depends on the gold and silver exports from the Americas. Metaphorical and mythological decor, the Baroque's peculiar verbal and iconographic alchemy, constitutes a kind of "theory of magic accumulation" that masks the real primitive accumulation of capital in the colonies and in the confiscation of Jewish and *morisco* property, making it appear harmonious with the religious and aristocratic assumptions of the state's imperialist ventures. As in the case of Góngora's *Angélica y Medoro*, such a procedure works to affirm the hegemony not by its *coincidence* with the official representations of power and authority but precisely by its defamiliarization of these. A poem like the *Soledades* or a novel like *Don Quijote* sets up a sphere of private experience that was distinct from but not (necessarily) in contradiction with the public sphere and the public identity of the reading subject as a social agent.

Maravall's thesis is that the Baroque was a kind of reactionary cultural populism directed against the ideological and social mobility in both Spain and Europe that threatened to break down both the hierarchical order of feudal estates and the authority of the church. As a "historical formation" (to use his term), it represents a feudalism that has incorporated and recontained the emerging energies of both a nascent bourgeois humanism and capitalism. Such a vision, however, entails a number of paradoxes. First, as J. H. Elliott, among others, has observed,[14] Maravall's concept of the absolutist state—which he derives from Weber's characterization of the modern state bureaucracy—assumes too great an identity of interests between Crown, nobility, and church, and too great a degree of centralization and functional rationalization of the state apparatus itself. (Elliott does not make the point, but it would be perhaps pertinent to his criticism to see the representation of the state in Baroque culture as the *imaginary*—in the Lacanian sense of a projection of desire that systematically misconstrues the real—of absolutism, rather than as a reflection of its actual coherence and authority.)

Second, if Baroque culture indeed seeks to reassert the principle of seigneurial authority, it cannot do this on a *purely feudal* or, what amounts to the same thing in culture, on a Scholastic basis. The Spanish literary Baroque is at least in part the product of the Jesuits' insistence that the suspect new genres of Renaissance vernacular literature, like the picaresque novel (which had been placed on the Index of Prohibited Books soon after it made its debut in the *Lazarillo de Tormes* in 1554), could be recuperated and mobilized in the service of post-Tridentine orthodoxy and the defense of Spain's overseas empire.[15] Among the products of the relative liberalization of literary policy that follows the death of Philip II in 1598 are *Don Quijote*, Góngora's *Polifemo* and *Soledades*, the *comedia*, and the body of novels known in Spanish literature as the Baroque picaresque.

What this implies, however, is that the literary forms the Baroque will mobilize against an emergent bourgeois and artisanal culture are precisely those provided by that culture: the Petrarchan lyric, the pastoral and picaresque novel, the essay, the autobiography, the prose *crónica* or "history," the plebian-humanist drama of the sort represented by the *Celestina* or Juan del Encina. Far from restoring the Scholastic principle of *comunitas*, based on the natural reciprocity of the hierarchically differentiated orders of society, Baroque culture tends precisely to interpellate the human subject as a solitary individual. Maravall notes that "in the baroque world individuals appear on the level of morality as monads," something confirmed by the picaresque novel or the "baroque anthropology" of Shakespeare's or Calderón's characters (203).

Third, the Baroque is a profoundly historicist cultural form. But its representation of history has a problematic dimension, since it addresses not only an apotheosis of empire but also a growing sense that Spain itself has entered its Iron Age, a period of irreversible crisis and decay. Elliott voices the question that must have inevitably confronted the Baroque *letrado*: "If all the great empires, including the greatest of them all, had risen only to fall, could Spain alone escape?" "The idea of an infinite cyclical process by which all living organisms were subject to growth, maturity and decay was deeply embedded in European thinking," he continues. "The organic conception of the state in the sixteenth century reinforced the analogy, and history confirmed it."[16] To represent history is to be aware of the possibility of change, but change is precisely something the Baroque—as an affirmation of the conservative sectors of Spanish society—wants to resist. How to deal with a situation in which history is seen both as a necessary, "epic" condition for sublimation and authority, and a force of decay or entropy that will reduce the architectonic consolidation of state and ecclesiastical power to the status of a ruin (or what is perhaps even more frightening and incomprehensible, bring to the fore in its further course new forms of human community and culture: that is, a new dominant class)? From this aporia derives the Baroque's peculiar fascination with ruins, disillusion (*desengaño*), and death.[17]

What is entailed in Baroque spiritualism as much as in Gracián's *conceptismo* is the paradoxical conjunction of the principle of submission to authority with the practical and theoretical ideal of the self-willed, independent individual. The quality of mind that is to synthesize these two aspects is *ingenio* or wit. Wit is what allows both for *desengaño*—the sense of the ultimate vanity of history and human desire—and for effective action and innovation in what Gracián called a "mundo trabucado," a world turned topsy-turvy, where both the expected forms and the foundations of value have become unstable. Wit is ultimately a political virtue and necessity, but it is to be learned primarily in the laboratory of poetic or artistic conceits. The artist is himself (much less frequently herself) in principle a *hidalgo* or gentleman, yet at the same time aware of the ambiguous nature of his or (problematically) her social position as a kind of artisan producing (sometimes for a living) a specific knowledge artifact. Góngora speaks of the *trabajo* or labor involved in both the creation and the reading of his poetry; Cervantes makes self-deprecating jokes about copyrights and royalties (both writers found themselves in severe financial difficulties); a favorite Baroque term is *fabricación*, making (the Spanish word for factory is *fábrica*; for a mechanically powered mill, *ingenio*); the formalized image of nature in Baroque landscape anticipates Newton's mechanics and Enlightenment deism. Partly as a consequence of a new sense of mastery and freedom, but partly also as a way of disassociating the artist from the sphere of ordinary labor and language, there arises something close to the modern ideology of the aesthetic, with its concepts of "genius" (a specifically aesthetic form of nobility) and aesthetic autonomy, which are tied in turn to the promotion of art by the ruling class as witness to its rule.

We may broach at this point the question of the role of the Baroque in the constitution of Latin American culture. According to Alejo Carpentier's influential slogan (in the preface to his novel *The Kingdom of This World*), Latin American literature is Baroque because the very nature of Latin American reality is Baroque. What is clear is that in the process of the Conquest the cultural models, like the language and religion, imposed by the Spanish in America (whose name is itself a Baroque conceit) represent a form of ethnocide, to use Pierre Clastres's concept.[18] In this sense, the appropriate model for the colonial Baroque would be more something like the cultural system of apartheid in South Africa than Carpentier's "real-marvelous" or the benevolent "mestizaje cultural" (cultural race-mixing) proposed by the founder of modern Latin American literary studies, Pedro Henríquez Ureña. For what counted as literature for the *peninsulares*, *conversos*, creoles, Indians, and mestizos who made up the population of colonial Spanish America was not only the colonial texts, like Alonso de Ercilla's *La Araucana* or Bernardo de Balbuena's *Grandeza mexicana*, written in or about America that we are accustomed to encountering in anthologies and histories of Latin American literature, but also most of the literary production of the Spanish Golden Age. The very acute sense of the power of literature that we have identified in the Spanish Baroque accounts, among other things, for the prohibition by the colonial authorities of both the publication and the importation of novels into the Americas. The novel was seen as a cultural form incompatible with the assumptions of colonial rule. It is true that this same overvalorization of literature in relation to power also made of it a cultural practice in which the ambitions and resentments of creole and mestizo—and in some cases Indian—groups could begin to articulate themselves in relation to the hegemony. But to what extent were the colonial *letrados* forwarding their own political-cultural agenda by taking up the practice of literature imposed during the Conquest? To what extent were they being co-opted by a Eurocentric agenda whose frontier agents they constituted?

The colonial *letrado*, creole or not, was in the position of having to mediate in his or her writing between an empirically vivid local reality and an increasingly absent and abstract center of metropolitan authority, represented in part by literary models. Even at a moment where, in its elaboration by writers like Cervantes or Góngora, literature was becoming a semiautonomous practice not directly related to "doctrine," literary problems of genre, style, decorum, neologism, and the like were prone to become entangled or confused with political and social problems; one of the results, as we have noted, is that literature itself became (and remains) a model and a medium at the same time for the constitution of the "national" in Latin America.

If, however, the Baroque has come to seem something like an *episteme* or "deep structure" of Latin American culture—a cultural modality in which its originality and anachronism can be recycled perpetually—the question still remains whether this inscription should be maintained. Is not the Baroque also a component of the cultural *neurosis* of Latin America in its (still-incomplete) stage of liberation struggle? The paradox of Spanish Baroque writing, both in the metropolis and the colonies, is that it was, like postmodernism today, at once a technique of power of a dominant class in a period of reaction and a figuration of the consciousness of the limits of that power. The other of the Baroque was consecutively Neoclassicism and political and economic liberalism—precisely the ideologies of the creole elites that led the independence struggle against Spanish domination in the early nineteenth century. Spain itself was, like Russia or the components of the Austro-Hungarian empire, a country that represented an impasse in the transition from feudalism to capitalism: hence the Black Legend and the anti-Baroque stance of the emerging bourgeois aesthetics. The other great culture of the Baroque was, of course, that of Counter-Reformation Italy, which had begun earlier and more powerfully than Spain the development of bourgeois culture only to reach a similar impasse. Of this impasse Gramsci noted acutely in the *Prison Notebooks* that in seventeenth-century Italy "Humanism assumed the aspect of a restoration. Yet like every restoration, it assimilated and developed, better than the revolutionary class it had politically suffocated, the ideological principles of the defeated class, which had not been able to go beyond its own corporate limits and create the superstructures of an integral society."[19] Hence the split between intelligentsia (whose crucial defining cultural practice becomes increasingly literature) and people that marks subsequent Italian cultural and political history.[20]

This does not exactly fit Spain, because of the populist and "national" character of Baroque culture there, although the point about the co-optation and involution of literary humanism by a Catholic and aristocratic intelligentsia is certainly relevant. Elliott warns against the tendency in Maravall to "overestimate the passivity of seventeenth-century societies and to exaggerate the capacity of those in authority to manipulate those societies for their own ideological ends. . . . The works of Spain's Golden Age contain sufficient ambiguities to suggest that subversive subtexts are there for the reading" (1987, 28).[21]

On the other hand, part of the literary Baroque's effectiveness as an ideological practice may have been precisely its ability to engage through ambiguities and possibilities of plural readings the attention and conviction of its audiences. As Foucault noted, "If power were never anything but repressive, if it never did anything but say no, do you really think one would be brought to obey it?"[22]

But since the Baroque is also, as Spengler argued in *The Decline of the West*, already partly the *modern*, let me close by noting that the place where the overvalorization of literature that it entails survives in the modern world is the academic practice of the humanities. The contemporary "man of letters" (of the "West") and contemporary literatures are carryovers from the Baroque into bourgeois-liberal culture, as is also the literary critic, who was brought into being in part by the demand for exegesis posed by the difficulty or novelty of the Baroque text. To reflect on the concept of the Spanish literary Baroque is thus also to reflect on the institution of literature and literary criticism itself in its function as an ideological apparatus of the state, that is, on the activity represented by this book.

Part II
Against Literature

CHAPTER 4

The Margin at the Center: On Testimonio

Do social struggles give rise to new forms of literature and culture, or is it more a question of the adequacy of their representation in existing forms? What happens when, as in the cases we have been considering, there has been a complicity between the form literature assumes in the Renaissance as a special kind of European cultural institution and the deployment of forms of colonial and imperialist oppression against which many of these struggles are directed? Are there experiences in the world today that would be betrayed or misrepresented by literature as we know it?

Raymond Williams formulated a similar set of concerns in relation to British working-class writing:

> Very few if any of us could write at all if certain forms were not available. And then we may be lucky, we may find forms which correspond to our experience. But take the case of the nineteenth-century working-class writers, who wanted to write about their working lives. The most popular form was the novel, but though they had marvelous material that could go into the novel very few of them managed to write good or any novels. Instead they wrote marvelous autobiographies. Why? Because the form coming down through the religious tradition was of a witness confessing the story of his life, or there was the defence speech at a trial when a man tells the judge who he is and what he had done, or of course other kinds of speech. These oral forms were more accessible forms centered on "I," on the single person. . . . The novel with its quite different narrative forms was virtually impenetrable to working-class writers for three or four generations, and there are still many problems in the received forms for what is, in the end, very different material. Indeed the forms of working-

class consciousness are bound to be different from the literary forms of another class, and it is a long struggle to find new and adequate forms.[1]

Let me set the frame of the discussion a bit differently: We have been considering how, in the period of what Marx described as the primitive accumulation in Western Europe—which is also the age of the rise of the bourgeoisie as a class and of the formation of the great colonial empires—there appear or reappear a series of new literary forms like the essay, the short story or *novela ejemplar*, the picaresque novel, the various kinds of Petrarchan lyric including the sonnet, the autobiography, and the new forms of secular theater, which become not only representations but also means of the emerging order. By the same token, we should expect an age such as our own—also one with at least the potential for transition from one mode of production to another—to evidence the emergence of new forms of cultural and literary expression that embody in a more or less thematically explicit and more or less formally articulated way the social forces that are contending for power in the world today. I have in mind here, by analogy to the role of the bourgeoisie in the transition from feudalism to capitalism, principally the struggle of working people everywhere against the domination of capital and the state, but also, in related ways, movements of ethnic or national liberation, the women's movement, poor and oppressed people's organizations of all types, the gay rights movement, the peace movement, ecological activism, and so on. One of these new forms in embryo, I will argue, is the kind of narrative text that in Latin American Spanish has come to be known as testimonio.

By testimonio, I mean a novel or novella-length narrative in book or pamphlet (that is, graphemic as opposed to acoustic) form, told in the first person by a narrator who is also the real protagonist or witness of the events she or he recounts. The unit of narration is usually a "life" or a significant life experience (for example, the experience of being a prisoner). Since, in many cases, the narrator is someone who is either functionally illiterate or, if literate, not a professional writer, the production of a testimonio often involves the tape recording and then the transcription and editing of an oral account by an interlocutor who is an intellectual, journalist, or writer. (To recall the Russian formalist term, testimonio is a sort of *skaz*, a literary simulacrum of oral narrative.) The nature of the intervention of this editorial function is one of the more hotly debated theoretical points in the discussion of the genre, and I will come back to it.

A variety of different kinds of texts—some of which would be considered literature, some not—can fit under the label of testimonio: for example, oral history, memoir, autobiography, chronicle, confession, life history, *novela-testimonio*, documentary novel, nonfiction novel, or "literature of fact." This makes it difficult to classify testimonio according to standard bibliographic categories. What section of a library or bookstore does a testimonio belong in? Under whose name is it to be listed in a card catalog or data base? How should it be reviewed: as a story or as a document? Since testimonio is by nature a demotic and dynamic form, not subject to critical legislation by a normative literary establishment, any attempt to specify a generic definition for it, as I do here, should be considered at best provisional, at worst repressive.

As Williams suggests, testimonio-like texts have been around for a long time, centered on the "I" and personal experience, and serving those subjects—the child, the "native," the woman, the insane, the criminal, the worker—for whom it was a matter of speaking or writing for themselves rather than being "spoken for." But for practical purposes, we can say that testimonio coalesced as a genre in the sixties, in close relation to the movements for national liberation and the generalized political and cultural radicalism of that decade. In Latin America, the event that sanctioned the testimonio as a genre or mode was the 1970 decision of Cuba's Casa de las Américas to begin awarding a prize in this category in its annual literary contest, and as we will see, something of the force of testimonio has to do with the new cultural and political practices opened up in the Americas by the Cuban Revolution.

The roots of testimonio go back to the importance in previous Latin American literature of a series of nonfictional narrative texts such as the colonial *crónicas* (Díaz del Castillo's *Verdadera Historia,* Cabeza de Vaca's *Naufragios);* the *costumbrista* "national" essay *(Facundo, Os sertões);* the war diaries *(diarios de campaña)* of military leaders like Bolívar or Martí; or the Romantic biographies of the heroes *(próceres)* of the nation, a key genre of Latin American liberalism. This tradition connected in the sixties with two other developments to produce the testimonio per se. One was the wide popularity of anthropological or sociological life histories composed from of tape-recorded narratives developed by academic social scientists like Oscar Lewis and Ricardo Pozas. The Cuban writer Miguel Barnet combined the model of the life history with the influence of Fernando Ortiz's ethnographic work on Afro-Cuban culture to produce perhaps the most influential of the "novela-testimonios," *Biografía de un cimarrón* (1966; in English, *The Autobiography of a Runaway Slave),* claiming that he was adding a literary dimension to what began simply as an ethnographic document.[2]

Testimonio also drew crucially on the popularity of direct-participant accounts of political and guerrilla activism, usually presented without literary pretensions, in particular Che Guevara's *Reminiscences of the Cuban Revolutionary War* (*Memorias de la guerra revolucionaria cubana*), one of the defining texts (along with its corresponding manual, *Guerrilla Warfare,* and Régis Debray's *Revolution in the Revolution?*) of sixties leftism throughout the Americas. On the model of the *Reminiscences,* there appear in Cuba in the early years after the revolution a series of narrative texts by or about combatants in Castro's 26th of July Movement and later in the campaigns against the counterrevolutionary bands in the Escambray mountains or at the Bay of Pigs. With the extension of *foquismo* as a strategy of armed struggle to countries like Venezuela, Guatemala, Nicaragua, Colombia, and Peru, a documentary literature centered on accounts of participation in guerrilla activity begins to appear all over Latin America, in part as a form of propaganda for armed struggle directed toward a potentially sympathetic reading public (students, young military officers, etc.), in part as a cadre literature internal to the revolutionary organizations themselves. Testimonio embraces many things besides first-person guerrilla narratives, but its emergence and prestige was clearly closely tied to armed struggles for national liberation in Latin America, and the Third World generally. (Thus, there is a Palestinian, Angolan, Irish, Brazilian, South African, and so on testimonial literature, but also U.S. texts like *The Autobiography of Malcolm X* or *Bury My Heart at Wounded Knee.*)[3]

An important element in the popularization of testimonio was the importance given in various forms of sixties counterculture to oral testimony as a form of personal authenticity, catharsis, and liberation: for example, the practice of "speaking bitterness" in the Chinese Cultural Revolution; Fanon's theory of decolonization; the consciousness-raising sessions of the early women's liberation movement; Laingian and, in a very different but not irrelevant way, Lacanian psychotherapies; and Paolo Freire's "pedagogy of liberation." Testimonio, in other words, is an instance of the feminist slogan "the personal is political."[4]

The word "testimonio" in Spanish suggests the act of testifying or bearing witness in a legal or religious sense. The connotation is important because it distinguishes testimonio from a simple recorded participant narrative or "oral history" (again, these distinctions are not intended to be absolute; how one reads a text is as important as what it is). In oral history it is the intentionality of the recorder—usually a social scientist or journalist—that is paramount; in testimonio, by contrast, it is the intentionality of the narrator. In René Jara's phrase, testimonio is a "narración de urgencia"—a story that *needs* to be told—involving a problem of repression, poverty, subalternity, exploitation, or simply survival that is implicated in the act of narration itself.[5] This suggests an affinity with the picaresque novel, particularly with that sense of the picaresque that sees the hero's act of telling his or her life as yet another picaresque act. But testimonio, even where it approximates in content a kind of neopicaresque, as it often does, is a fundamentally different narrative mode. It is not, to begin with, "fiction." We are meant to experience as real both the speaker and the situations and events recounted. The legal-religious connotation implicit in its convention implies a pledge of honesty or sincerity on the part of the narrator that the interlocutor/reader is bound to respect, and the assumed lack of writing ability or skill on the part of the narrator, even in those cases where the story is written instead of told orally, contributes further to the "truth effect" of testimonio. The reception of testimonio thus has something to do with a revulsion for fiction and the fictive as such, with its postmodernist estrangement perhaps.

Moreover, testimonio is not so much concerned with the life of (to borrow Lukács's phrase) a "problematic hero" like the picaro as with a problematic collective social situation that the narrator lives alongside others. The situation of the narrator in testimonio must be representative (in both the mimetic and the legal-political senses) of a larger social class or group; in the picaresque novel, by contrast, a collective social predicament such as unemployment and marginalization is experienced and narrated as a personal destiny. Even where the narrator in the testimonio is of upper- or middle-class background, the situation he or she recounts must involve in some sense or other a loss of the privilege and privacy that separates him or her from subaltern social groups: for example, in the experience of prison or political repression. The "I" that speaks to us in the picaresque novel or the first-person bildungsroman is precisely the mark of a difference or antagonism with the community, what Jauss called the *Ichform* of the self-made man.[6] The narrator in testimonio, on the other hand, speaks for or in the name of a community or group, approximating in this way the symbolic function of the epic hero without at the same time assuming his hierarchical and patriarchal status. Jara speaks of an "epicidad cotidiana," an everyday epicality, in the testimonio. Another way of putting this would be to define testimonio as a nonfictional, popular-democratic form of epic narrative.

By way of example, these are the opening lines of *I, Rigoberta Menchú*:

> My name is Rigoberta Menchú. I am twenty-three years old.
> This is my testimony. I didn't learn it from a book and I didn't
> learn it alone. I'd like to stress that it's not only my life, it's
> also the testimony of my people. It's hard for me to remember
> everything that's happened to me in my life since there have

been many bad times but, yes, moments of joy as well. The important thing is that what has happened to me has happened to many other people also: My story is the story of all poor Guatemalans. My personal experience is the reality of a whole people.[7]

As her selection for the Nobel Peace Prize in 1992 ratifies, Rigoberta Menchú has been an activist for her people, the Quiché Indians of the western highlands of Guatemala. At the time she gave her testimonio, she was working for the Committee of Campesino Unity (CUC); her father had been a founder of the CUC and one of the demonstrators killed by the army in the widely reported occupation of the Spanish embassy; and her mother and brother had been recently killed by the army as political activists in the counterinsurgency campaign of the early eighties. So this statement is perhaps a little more explicit than is usual in a testimonio. But the metonymic function of the narrative voice the statement implies—its power to stand in for the experience of the community as a whole—is latent in the form; it is part of the narrative contract it establishes with the reader. Even in those cases where the narrator speaks from a "marginal" social position (as a prostitute or drug addict, for example), the private history always confronts the reader with larger issues of social justice.

Unlike traditional epic, which depends on the hero's having a higher status than the reader or listener, testimonio is a fundamentally democratic and egalitarian form of narrative in the sense that it implies that *any* life so narrated can have a kind of representativity. Each individual testimonio evokes an absent polyphony of other voices, other possible lives and experiences. Thus, one common formal variation on the classic first-person testimonio is the polyphonic testimonio made up of accounts by different participants in the same event or social group.[8]

What testimonio does have in common with the picaresque novel and with autobiography is the powerful textual affirmation of the speaking subject itself. This should be evident in the passage from *I, Rigoberta Menchú* just quoted. The dominant formal aspect of the testimonio is that voice which speaks to the reader in the form of an "I" that demands to be recognized, that wants or needs to stake a claim on our attention. This presence of the voice, which we are meant to experience as the voice of a real rather than fictional person, is the mark of a desire not to be silenced or defeated, to impose oneself on an institution of power like literature from the position of the excluded or the marginal. Jameson has argued that testimonio produces a "new anonymity," a form of selfhood distinct from the "overripe subjectivity" of the modernist bildungsroman.[9] But this way of thinking about testimonio runs the risk of conceding to its subjects of enunciation only the facelessness that is already theirs in the dominant culture. We should note, rather, the insistence on and affirmation of the authority of the subject evident in titles like *I, Rigoberta Menchú* (even more strongly in the Spanish: *Me llamo Rigoberta Menchú y así me nació la conciencia*); *I'm a Juvenile Delinquent* (*Soy un delincuente*); *Let Me Speak! Testimony of Domitila, a Woman of the Bolivian Mines* (*Si me permiten hablar*); *Doris Tijerino: Inside the Nicaraguan Revolution* (*"Somos milliones": La vida de Doris María*).[10]

In a related way, testimonio implies a challenge to the loss of the authority of orality in the context of processes of cultural modernization that privilege literacy and literature as a norm of expression. It permits the entry into literature of persons who would normally—in those societies (most) where literature is a form of class privilege—be excluded from direct literary expression, who have had to be "represented" by professional writers. There is a crucial difference in power terms between having someone like Rigoberta Menchú tell the story of her people (and win a Nobel Prize herself) and having it told, however well, by someone like the Nobel Prize-winning Guatemalan novelist Miguel Ángel Asturias.

As I noted in my comparison of *I, Rigoberta Menchú* with Richard Rodriguez's *Hunger of Memory* in chapter 1, testimonio involves an erasure of the function and thus also of the textual presence of the "author," which by contrast is so powerfully present in all major forms of bourgeois writing since the Renaissance, so much so that our very notions of literature and the literary are bound up with notions of the author, or of an authorial "intention." In Miguel Barnet's phrase, the author has been replaced in testimonio by the function of a "compiler" (*compilador*) or "activator" (*gestante*), somewhat on the model of the film producer. Implicit in this is both a challenge and an alternative to the patriarchal and elitist function the author plays in class and sexually and racially divided societies, and in particular to the concept of the "great writer" or artist as culture hero that is so deeply embedded in the ideology of modernism generally and in the institution of literature in Latin America in particular.

The erasure of authorial presence in the testimonio, together with its nonfictional character, make possible a different kind of complicity—we might call it fraternal or sororal—between narrator and reader than is possible in the novel, which, as Lukács showed in *Theory of the Novel*, usually entails an ironic distancing on the part of both novelist and reader from the fate of the protagonist. Eliana Rivero, writing about *La montaña es algo más que una inmensa estepa verde*, a testimonio by the Sandinista guerrilla comandante Omar Cabezas (published in English as *Fire from the Mountain*), notes that "the act of speaking faithfully recorded on the tape, transcribed and then 'written' remains in the testimonio punctuated by a repeated series of interlocutive and conversational markers . . . which constantly put the reader on alert, so to speak: True? Are you following me? OK? So?" She concludes that the testimonio is a "snail-like discourse (*discurso encaracolado*) which turns on itself and which in the process totally deautomatizes the reaction of the reader, whose complicity it invites through the medium of his or her counterpart in the text, the direct interlocutor."[11]

Just as testimonio implies a new kind of relation between narrator and reader, the contradictions of gender, class, race, and age that frame the narrative's production can also reproduce themselves in the relation of the narrator to this direct interlocutor, especially when it is the case, as in *I, Rigoberta Menchú*, that the narrator is someone who requires an interlocutor with a different ethnic and/or class background in order first to elicit the oral account, then to give it textual form as a testimonio, and then to see to its publication and distribution.[12]

I do not want to minimize the nature of these contradictions; among other things, they represent the possibility for a reactionary articulation of testimonio as a sort of *costum-brismo* of the subaltern, or for the smothering of a genuine popular voice by well-intentioned but repressive notions of political correctness or pertinence. Conversely, the relation established between narrator and compiler in the production of a testimonio can serve as both an allegorical figure for, and a concrete form of, the political alliance of a radicalized intelligentsia with the "people" that has been decisive in the development of resistance movements. Put another way, the testimonio gives voice in literature to a previously "voiceless" and anonymous popular-democratic subject, but in such a way that the intellectual or professional—usually of bourgeois or petty-bourgeois background—is interpellated, in his or her function as interlocutor/reader of the testimonio, as being in alliance with (and to some extent dependent on) this subject, without at the same time losing his or her identity as an intellectual. Testimonio is not a form of liberal guilt, in other words. It suggests as an appropriate ethical and political response more the possibility of solidarity than of charity.

Generally speaking, the audience for testimonio, either in the immediate national or local context or in metropolitan cultural centers, remains that "reading public" which, in presocialist societies—and even in the "advanced" capitalist democracies—is still gender- and class-limited. The complicity a testimonio establishes with its readers involves their identification—by engaging their standards of ethics and justice in a speech-act situation that requires response—with a cause normally distant, not to say alien, from their immediate experience. Testimonio in this sense has been important in maintaining and developing the practice of human rights and solidarity movements, both within regions and countries and in transnational circuits of cultural representation.

Rigoberta Menchú's direct interlocutor was Elisabeth Burgos-Debray, a Venezuelan social scientist living in Paris, with all that implies about contradictions between metropolis and periphery, high and low culture, dominant and emergent social formations, dominant and subaltern languages. Her account of the relationship she developed with

Rigoberta Menchú in the course of doing the testimonio forms the preface to the book, constituting a sort of testimonio about the production of a testimonio. One of the problems the two women encountered is that Menchú had to speak to Burgos-Debray in Spanish, the language for her of the *ladinos* (in Guatemala, Spanish-speaking whites or mestizos) who oppressed her people, which she had just and very imperfectly learned (the conflict in Guatemala between Spanish and indigenous languages is, in fact, one of the themes of her narrative). In preparing the text, Burgos-Debray had to decide, then, what to correct and what not in Menchú's recorded speech. She left in, for example, repetitions and digressions that she considered characteristic of oral narrative. On the other hand, she decided to correct "the gender mistakes which inevitably occur when someone has just learned to speak a foreign language. It would have been artificial to leave them uncorrected and it would have made Rigoberta look 'picturesque', which is the last thing I wanted" (xx–xxi).

The relation that Rigoberta Menchú and Elisabeth Burgos-Debray establish in the production of the testimonio in one sense enacts the relationship of humanism itself to subaltern cultures: it entails thus the possibility, in the manner familiar from the dialectic of master and slave, of the compiler manipulating the material the informant provides to suit her own political, intellectual, and aesthetic predilections, which are not necessarily those of the informant. K. Millet makes the following argument about the testimonio of a Mapuche woman, Lucinda Nahuelhual, compiled by the Chilean feminist activist Sonia Montecino Aguirre:

> *Los sueños de Lucinda Nahuelhual* is not a narrative about a Mapuche Indian woman, but rather it is a textualizing of Ms. Sonia Montecino Aguirre and her political sympathies. . . . From the moment of the narrative's inception, the figure of "the other," Lucinda Nahuelhual, is only that, a figure, an empty signifier, a narration constructed on the significations of Ms. Aguirre's own political agenda. . . . the idea of "elevating" the Mapuche woman, Lucinda, to the status of a signifier of an urban feminist movement where power is maintained primarily within the hands of "enlightened"

women from the hegemony requires that the indigenous
woman accept a position of loss in order to signify meaning to
her audience of "sisters."[13]

Although it is true that there are possibilities of distortion
and misrepresentation involved in testimonio, Millet's argument seems to reject the possibility of any textual representation of an "other" as such in favor of something like a (liberal?) notion of the irreducible particularity of the individual
(all signifiers are "empty" unless and until they signify
something for somebody, somebody being, of course, another signifier). In a context such as that of Chile under the
Pinochet dictatorship, the strategic political question would
seem to be not so much to insist on the *difference* in the situations of a Mapuche woman and an urban, middle-class
feminist movement, but rather on the possibility of their articulation together in a common program or front that could
at the same time advance women's rights and the rights of
indigenous groups, without subordinating one to another.

What happens in testimonio is not only the conversion of
an "other" into an ideological signifier but also the confrontation through the text of one person (the reader and/or interlocutor) with another at the level of a *possible* solidarity
and unity (a unity in which differences will be respected).
In the creation of the testimonial text, information and control of representation do not just flow one way: someone like
Rigoberta Menchú is also manipulating her metropolitan interlocutor in order to have her story reach and influence an
international audience, something that, as an activist for her
community, she sees in quite utilitarian terms as a political
task. Moreover, editorial power does not belong to the compiler alone. Menchú, worrying—correctly—that there are
some ways in which making her narrative available as "literature" could be used against herself or her people (for example, by academic specialists advising counterinsurgency
programs such as those the CIA and the Israeli Defense
Forces set up in Guatemala), notes that there are certain
things—her Nahuatl name, for example—that she will *not*
speak of.[14] Although Burgos-Debray does the final sequenc-
ing, the narrative units are wholly composed by Menchú

and, as such, depend for their effect on her skills and intentions as a narrator. An example of this may be found in the excruciating detail she uses (in chapters 24 and 27 of her book) to describe the torture and murder of her brother and mother by the Guatemalan army, a form of figuration that gives these episodes a hallucinatory and symbolic intensity different from the matter-of-fact narration one expects from testimonio. One could say that this is a kind of testimonial expressionism or "magic realism."

Perhaps something like Mao's idea of "contradictions among the people" (as opposed to contradictions between "the people" as a whole and, say, imperialism in the case of a foreign occupation)[15] best captures the nature of the relations between narrator, interlocutor-compiler, and reader in the testimonio, in the sense that there are deep and inescapable contradictions involved in these relations, contradictions that can only be resolved on the level of general structural change on both national and global levels, but also a sense of sisterhood and mutuality in the struggle against a common system of oppression. Testimonio is not intended to be, in other words, a reenactment of the anthropological function of the colonial or subaltern native informant. That is why although one of the sources of the testimonio is the ethnographic life history of the *Children of Sánchez* sort, it is not reducible to that category, nor to oral history as forms of information retrieval on the subaltern.[16]

One thing evident in the passage from *I, Rigoberta Menchú* that we have been discussing is that the presence of a "real" subaltern voice in the testimonio is in part an illusion; we are dealing here—as in any discursive medium—with an effect that has been produced, in the case of a testimonio by both the direct narrator—using devices of an oral storytelling tradition—and the compiler, who, according to literary norms of narrative form and decorum, makes a text out of the material. Although it is easy to deconstruct this illusion, it is also necessary to insist on it to understand the testimonio's peculiar aesthetic-ideological power. Elzbieta Sklodowska, developing a point about the textual nature of testimonio that can be connected with Millet's critique of testimonio noted earlier, cautions that it would be naive to assume a direct homology between text and history. The discourse of a witness cannot be a reflection of his or her experience, but rather a refraction determined by the vicissitudes of memory, intention, ideology. The intention and the ideology of the author-editor further superimpose the original text, creating more ambiguities, silences, and absences in the process of selecting and editing the material in a way consonant with norms of literary form. Thus, although the testimonio uses a series of devices to gain a sense of veracity and authenticity—among them the point of view of the first-person witness-narrator—the play between fiction and history reappears inexorably as a problem.[17]

What is at stake, however, is the particular nature of the "truth effect" of testimonio, not simply the difference between (any) text and reality. Testimonio produces if not the real as such (in the Lacanian sense of that which resists symbolization absolutely), then certainly a sensation of *experiencing the real* that, for example, even news reports do not. "More than an interpretation of reality," notes René Jara in a tacit response to Sklodowska, the testimonio is "*a trace of the real*, of that history which, as such, is inexpressible" (2).

Sklodowska is right in some sense about the "play" between history and fiction (and narrator and interlocutor) in testimonio. But to simply subsume testimonio under the category of literary fictionality is to deprive it of its power to engage the reader in the ways I have indicated, to make of it another (an-Other?) form of literature. This seems a formalist and, at least in effect, a "liberal" response to testimonio that tolerates or encourages its incorporation into modern literature—where it can become another item of postmodern cultural consumption—at the expense of relativizing the moral and political urgency demanded by the real-life referent it narrates. What has to be understood instead is how testimonio radically puts into question the existing institution of literature as a form of class, race, and gender privilege at the same time that it constitutes itself as something like a new literary genre.[18]

Is testimonio really something new under the sun? How—or why—does one distinguish it from autobiography and/or cognate forms of personal narrative like memoirs, diaries, confessions, or reminiscences? The dividing line is not always exact, but the following might represent the general case: Even in nineteenth-century memoirs of women or ex-slaves (that is, texts where the narrator writes from a subaltern position), there is implicit an ideology of individualism in the very convention of the autobiographical form, which is built on the notion of a coherent, self-evident, self-conscious commanding subject who appropriates literature precisely as a means of "self-expression," and who in turn constructs textually for the reader the liberal imaginary of a unique, "free," autonomous ego as the natural form of being and public achievement. By contrast, in testimonio the "I" has the grammatical status of what linguists call a "shifter"—a linguistic function that can be assumed indiscriminately by anyone. Recalling Rigoberta Menchú's narrative proposition, the meaning of her testimonio lies not in the uniqueness of her self or experience but in its ability to stand for the experience of her community as a whole.

Just as the authorial function has been erased or mitigated in testimonio, so too the relationship between authorship and forms of individual and hierarchical power in bourgeois society is shifted. Testimonio is an affirmation of the authority of a single speaking subject, even of personal awareness and growth, but it cannot affirm a self-identity that is separate from a group or class situation marked by marginalization, oppression, and struggle. If it does this, it ceases to be testimonio and becomes in effect autobiography, that is, as in Rodriguez's *Hunger of Memory*, both an account of and a means of access to middle- or upper-class status, a sort of documentary bildungsroman. Even where its subject is a person "of the left," as, for example, in Agnes Smedley's *Daughter of Earth* or Pablo Neruda's *Memoirs*, autobiography and autobiographical novels are essentially conservative modes in the sense that they imply that individual triumph over circumstances is possible, in spite of "obstacles," that it is a matter of will and dedication. (If Rigoberta Menchú had become a writer instead of remaining as she has a member of and an activist for her ethnic community, her narrative would be autobiography.) Autobiography produces in the reader (who, generally speaking, is already either middle- or upper-class or looking to be) the specular effect of confirming and authorizing his or (less so) her situation of relative social privilege. Testimonio—even testimonios from the political right like Armando Valladares's Cuban prison memoir, *Against All Hope*, or Solzhenitsyn's *Gulag Archipelago*—on the other hand, always signifies the need for a general social change in which the stability of the reader's world must be brought into question.[19]

If the novel is a closed and private form in the sense that both the story and the subject end with the end of the text, defining that autoreferential self-sufficiency which is the basis of formalist reading practices, the testimonio by contrast exhibits what Jara calls a "public intimacy," in which the boundary between literature and real life, public and private spheres, essential in all forms of bourgeois culture and law, is transgressed. The narrator in testimonio is a real person who continues living and acting in a real social history, which also continues. Testimonio can never, in this sense, create the illusion of that textual in-itselfness, set against and above the everyday life and struggle, that is the basis of literary formalism. Nor can it be adequately analyzed by close-reading or textual deconstruction. It is, to borrow Umberto Eco's slogan, an "open work," which implies the importance and power of literature as a form of social action, but also its radical insufficiency. In principle, testimonio appears therefore as an extraliterary or even antiliterary form of discourse.

What happens, then, when something like testimonio *becomes* literature? Does this involve a neutralization of its peculiar aesthetic-ideological effect, which depends, as we have seen, on its status outside accepted literary genres and norms? If the picaresque novel was the psuedoautobiography of a lower-class individual (thus inverting a "learned" humanist form into a pseudopopular one), we may observe in recent literature (1) novels that are in fact pseudotestimonios, like Manlio Argueta's re-creation of the world of a peasant mother in El Salvador, *Un día en la vida* (One Day of Life), or Luis Zapata's *El vampiro de la colonia Roma*, which purports to be the tape-recorded memoirs of a homosexual prostitute in Mexico City; (2) a growing concern with reproducing something like a testimonial voice in the novel, in, for example, Gabriel García Márquez's *Crónica de una muerte anunciada* (Chronicle of a Death Foretold) or Mario Vargas Llosa's *Historia de Mayta* (The Story of Mayta); (3) narrative texts located ambiguously between the authorial novel and testimonio, like Raúl Walsh's *Operación masacre*, Nawal El Saadawi's *Woman at Point Zero*, Elena Poniatowska's *Hasta no verte Jesús mío* and Miguel Barnet's *Canción de Rachel* (the last three fictionalizations of actual testimonial material), or Yang Jiang's *A Cadre School Life*, which is a testimonio of the author's experiences in the Cultural Revolution rendered in the mold of a narrative genre of classical Chinese literature.

In literary history, the intensification of a narrative or representational "reality effect" is generally associated with the contestation of the dominant system and its forms of cultural idealization and legitimation. This was certainly the case of the early bourgeois novel in relation to the idealist genres of late-feudal narrative; for example, the corrosive irony of *Don Quijote* or the crude realism of the picaresque novel vis-à-vis the novels of chivalry. In fact, the realist novel is assimilated in orthodox Aristotelian Renaissance literary theory only with some difficulty (because its domain is the mundane and the particular rather than the universal and the beautiful). In like fashion, if testimonio necessarily appears at the margin of literature, it is also on the way to becoming a new form of literature, with significant cultural and political repercussions. To return to our starting point: if the novel has had a special relationship with humanism and the rise of the European bourgeoisie and with colonialism and imperialism (and thus with the founding of the conditions of social oppression and inequality that testimonio represents), testimonio is, by contrast, a new form of literary narrative in which we can at the same time witness and be a part of the emerging culture of an international proletarian/popular-democratic subject in its period of ascendancy and struggle for hegemony. But it would be in the spirit of testimonio itself to end on a more skeptical note (which may also serve as an entry point for the subsequent essay): literature, even where it is infused with a popular-democratic form and content, as in the case of testimonio, is not itself a popular-democratic cultural form, and (*pace* Gramsci) it is an open question as to whether it can ever be. How much of a favor do we do testimonio by positing, as I do here, that it is a new form of literary narrative or by making it an alternative reading to the canon, as in case of the Stanford general education requirement? Perhaps such moves preempt or occlude a vision of an emergent popular-democratic culture that is no longer based on the institutions of humanism and literature.

CHAPTER 5

Second Thoughts on Testimonio

What separates the discussion of testimonio in this chapter from the last is the fact of the defeat of the Sandinistas in the February 1990 elections in Nicaragua, which reminds us of Jameson's redefinition of Lacan's category of the Real as that which hurts. A decade after the revolutionary high tide of 1979–81, it is clear that the moment of optimism about the possibilities for rapid social transformation in Central America has passed. Whether this represents a new, postrevolutionary stage in that region (or for that matter the world), or simply a recession before the appearance of a new cycle of radicalization—perhaps also involving Mexico this time—is open to question. Testimonios like *I, Rigoberta Menchú*, Omar Cabezas's *Fire from the Mountain*, or Margaret Randall's *Sandino's Daughters* were a vital part of the literary imaginary of international solidarity with or critical support for the Central American revolutions. So the electoral defeat of the Sandinistas, while it is certainly not absolute—unlike Chile after the defeat of Allende, there is still room for maneuver and struggle— must force us in any case to reconsider the links between testimonio, liberation struggles, and academic pedagogy. I want to center this reconsideration in particular around the question of the relation of testimonio to the field of literature. This will in turn connect with some questions about what it is that we do in the humanities generally, and particularly in connection with Latin American and third world literatures.

Testimonios like *I, Rigoberta Menchú* are made for people like us in that they allow us to participate as academics and yuppies, without leaving our studies and classrooms, in the concreteness and relativity of actual social struggles ("us" and "our" designate the readers—or potential readers—of this book). I am not trying to guilt trip people about being academics and yuppies; I am both (perhaps more muppie than yuppie). I believe in Gramsci's slogan of a long march through the institutions, and it follows that our battlefield is the classroom and conference hall, that the struggle over the teaching and interpretation of literature has something to do with the production of new forms of ideological hegemony. As a pedagogic issue, the use of testimonio in the classroom has to do with the possibility of interpellating our students in a relation of solidarity with liberation movements and human rights struggles, both here in the United States and abroad.

I noted in chapter 4 that much deconstructive zeal has been spent on the fact that testimonio is a mediated narrative: as in the case of *I, Rigoberta Menchú*, usually an oral narrative told by a speaker from a subaltern or "popular" social class or group to an interlocutor who is an intellectual or professional writer from the middle or upper class (and, in many cases, from a different ethnolinguistic position: the equivalent of what Peruvians call a *pituco*—white, affluent, culturally European, etc.), who then edits and textualizes the account, making it available to a similarly positioned national and international reading public as a printed book or pamphlet. The possibilities of distortion and/or co-optation in the production and reception of testimonio are many, as Gayatri Spivak's question "Can the subaltern speak?" invites us to consider. Latin American literature has an extensive gallery of subalterns who "speak" to the hegemony: the Indian *traductores* (translators) of the Conquest, like Cortés's mistress, La Malinche; "good slaves" like Francisco in the Cuban antislavery novels of the nineteenth century; the peasant in Central American *costumbrismo* (which, in Sergio Ramírez's phrase, "saw the countryside from the balcony"); women characters generally, in both nineteenth-century oligarchic romances and the modernist narrative of the Boom (Doña Bárbara's daughter, if not Doña Bárbara herself); the "native informants" of both traditional and contemporary ethnography. Nor does it help much that this subject appears now shrouded in the latest twists and turns of post-structuralist theory, because, as Spivak notes, "contemporary invocations of 'libidinal economy' and desire as the determining interest, combined with the practical politics of the oppressed (under socialized capital) 'speaking for themselves,' restore the category of the sovereign subject within the theory that seems most to question it."[1]

Is testimonio, then, simply a new chapter in an old history of the literary "relations" between dominant and exploited classes and groups, metropolis and colony, center and periphery, First and Third Worlds? Is it yet another version of a subaltern subject who gives us now—in addition to the surplus value her exploitation in the new circuits of global capital produces—something we desire perhaps even more in these times of the political economy of the sign: her "truth," a truth that is, as stated at the start of *I, Rigoberta Menchú*, "the reality of a whole people" ("toda la realidad de un pueblo")?[2]

I had a chance to meet Rigoberta Menchú personally at a talk she gave at New York University in 1989. She looked very much the way her interlocutor, Elisabeth Burgos-Debray had described her in the introduction to the book some ten years earlier:

> She was wearing traditional costume, including a
> multicoloured *huipil* with rich and varied embroidery. . . . The
> first thing that struck me about her was her open, almost
> child-like smile. Her face was round and moon-shaped. Her
> expression was as guileless as that of a child and a smile
> hovered permanently on her lips. (xiv)

But I had not spent a good part of my youth in left-wing organizations of one sort or another not to be able to recognize behind this image (which might well serve as an advertisement for Guatemalan embroideries or tourist agencies) the at once inspiring and intimidating figure of the *organizer*. Because in spite of that textual metonymy in the testimonio that equates individual life history with the history of a group or people, testimonial narrators like Rigoberta Menchú are not exactly the subaltern as such—Spivak is correct that the subaltern cannot speak in this sense; they are rather something more like "organic intellectuals" of the subaltern who can speak to the hegemony by means of this metonymy of self in the name and in the place of it.

What, after all, was the daughter of Mayan peasants from the Guatemalan highlands doing speaking to an audience of yuppie professors and students at New York University anyway? The reception of testimonio today is bound up with the globalization of both capitalist exploitation and the new forms of resistance to it, and thus traverses directly that center of information retrieval and knowledge production which is the university. Testimonio both allegorizes and embodies the possibility of regional, national, and/or transnational coalitions of radicalized intellectuals and professionals with subaltern classes or social groups; it is a form of a global "alliance politics" of the left. As Doris Sommer observes: "to read women's testimonials, curiously, is to mitigate the tension between First World self and Third World other. I do not mean this as a license to deny the differences, but as a suggestion that the testimonial subject may be a model for respectful, nontotalizing, politics."[3]

Testimonios like *I, Rigoberta Menchú* are not only *representations* of new forms of subaltern resistance and struggle but also models and even *means* for these. In the context of the university, understood both as an institution of the "West" and of class power, testimonios are almost literally "foreign agents"—which is why, as I noted in chapter 1, the figure of Rigoberta Menchú and the scandal of the assignment of her testimonio in one of the courses of the Stanford general education requirement became a central focus for the neoconservative assault on multicultural education and political correctness.

I understand, of course, that "literature" is itself a matter of semiosis, of who defines what counts and under what institutional circumstances. The political question is what is gained or lost by including or excluding under this name any particular kind of discursive practice. As in the Stanford case, the pedagogic incorporation of testimonio in the academy has involved strategically a theoretical-critical struggle to define it not just as an ethnographic document or "life history" but as part of the canon of Great Works through which the humanist subject as such is formed in a modern, multicultural curriculum. The authorizing operation of literary criticism and theory (including, of course, my own construction of testimonio as a genre) in this regard has been to articulate testimonio as a form of "minor" literature particularly sensitive to the representation or expression of subalternity. Thus, Alan Carey Webb, who has taught an undergraduate course on world literature at the University of Oregon based entirely on testimonios, notes that *I, Rigoberta Menchú*

> is one of the most moving books I have ever read. It is the kind of a book that I feel I must pass on, that I must urge fellow teachers to use in their classes. . . . My students were immediately sympathetic to Menchú's story and were anxious to know more, to involve themselves. They asked questions about culture and history, about their own position in the world, and about the purposes and methods of education. Many saw in the society of the Guatemalan Indian attractive features they found lacking in their own lives, strong family relationships, community solidarity, an intimate relationship with nature, commitment to others and to one's beliefs.[4]

Jameson gives testimonio his imprimatur as an alternative to what he terms the "overripe subjectivity" of the bildungsroman; Barbara Harlow makes it a key form of antiimperialist narrative in her *Resistance Literature*; Cornell University Press publishes Barbara Foley's book on "documentary fiction" mentioned in chapter 4; Margaret Randall offers a "how to" manual for would-be practitioners of the form; George Yúdice postulates it as a third world form of a postmodernism of resistance; Gayatri Spivak and Elzbieta Sklodowska caution against a naive reception of the form; and so on.[5] Even to arrive at the situation we are now in, where it has become fashionable to deconstruct, in de Manian fashion, this or that testimonio—Roberto González Echevarría pioneered this in his article on Miguel Barnet's *Autobiography of a Runaway Slave*[6]—is still to give testimonio in effect status as a literary text comparable to, say, Rousseau's *Confessions*.

This is fine and basically correct, as far as I am concerned. There is no reason to suppose that Rousseau has anything more or less to tell us than Rigoberta Menchú or Esteban Montejo, the narrator of the *Autobiography of a Runaway Slave*. But we must also understand why testimonio comes

into being outside or at the margin of the historically constituted institution of literature in modern Western culture. As
I noted earlier, at least part of the aesthetic effect of testimonio—in the Russian formalist sense of *ostranenie* or defamiliarization—is paradoxically that it is *not* literary, not
linguistically elaborated or authorial. One symptom of this
has been an ambivalence about the "artistic" as opposed to
the "documentary" character of testimonio, and about the
distinction between testimonio per se and the more elaborated "testimonial novel" (*novela-testimonio*) such as those of
Miguel Barnet (Truman Capote's *In Cold Blood* would be an
English-language equivalent).[7] Testimonio appears where
the adequacy of existing literary forms and styles—even of
the dominant language itself—for the representation of the
subaltern has entered into crisis.[8] Even where its instrumentality is to reach in printed form a metropolitan reading public culturally and physically distant from the position and
situation of its narrator, testimono is not engendered out of
the same humanist ideology of the literary that motivates its
reception by this public or its incorporation into the humanities curriculum. What is more (as is often the case with the
subaltern), it seems positively ungrateful about its accep-
tance at places like Stanford, at times even actively resisting
the attempt to make it "literature." Let me give two examples, the first from a testimonio of the armed struggle in
El Salvador in the 1970s, the second from *I, Rigoberta
Menchú*.

Ana Guadalupe Martínez's memoir *Las cárceles clandestinas
de El Salvador* (The Secret Prisons of El Salvador) deals with
her involvement in the Salvadoran guerrilla underground
with the Ejército Revolucionario del Pueblo (Revolutionary
Army of the People) and her capture, torture, and impris-
onment by the army. She insists that the account she gives
is "the result of a collective and militant effort, and *has no
intellectual or literary pretensions*; it is a contribution to the ideological development and formation of cadres on the basis
of concrete experience that should be discussed and analyzed by those who are consistently immersed in the making
of the revolution." Her coprologuist similarly notes: "There
is considerable concrete experience that has been lost by not
being processed and transmitted by militants, and another

large part has been deformed in its essence by being elaborated by leftist intellectual intermediaries who adjust what they are relating not in relation to revolutionary needs but *in relation to the needs of fiction and bourgeois revolutionary theorizing.*"[9]

The point about "no intellectual pretensions" is disingenuous, and there is more than a trace here of the intense sectarianism that has marked the Salvadoran revolutionary movement. The reference to "leftist intellectual intermediaries" alludes to El Salvador's most well-known modern writer, Roque Dalton, who also worked in testimonial forms,[10] and who, as it happens, was Martínez's adversary in an internal debate in the ERP in the mid-seventies over the direction of the armed struggle (a debate that led to his assassination by the leadership faction of the ERP that Martínez apppears to have supported). Still, her point is worth taking. She wants to do something *other than* literature with her narrative, feels it would in some sense be compromised or betrayed by becoming literature, whereas Dalton, like Miguel Barnet, was concerned with the ideological and aesthetic problems of making testimonio a form of left-modernist literature.

I, Rigoberta Menchú begins, you may recall, with a strategic disavowal of both literature and the liberal concept of the authority of private experience that literature implies: "My name is Rigoberta Menchú. I am twenty three years old. This is my testimony. I didn't learn it from a book and I didn't learn it alone" (1). This quote belongs with a series of passages where the narrator explicitly counterposes book learning to direct experience, or attacks the presence of no doubt well-intentioned schoolteachers in her village, arguing that they represent an agency of penetration and destruction of the highland Indian communities by the landowners and the Guatemalan state. Here are some examples:

> When children reach ten years old [in our village], that's the moment when their parents and the village leaders talk to them again. . . . It's also when they remind them that our ancestors were dishonored by the White Man, by colonization. But they don't tell them the way it's written down in books, because the majority of Indians can't read or write, and don't even know that they have their own texts. No, they learn it

through oral recommendations, the way it has been handed down through the generations. (13)

I had a lot of ideas but I knew I couldn't express them all. I wanted to read or write Spanish. I told my father this, that I wanted to learn to read. Perhaps things were different if you could learn to read. My father said, "Who will teach you? You have to find out by yourself, because I can't help you. I know of no schools and I have no money for them anyway." I told him that if he talked to the priests, perhaps they'd give me a scholarship. But my father said he didn't agree with that idea because I was trying to leave the community, to go far away, and find out what was best for me. He said: "You'll forget about our common heritage." . . . My father was very suspicious of schools and all that sort of thing. He gave as an example the fact that many of my cousins had learned to read and write but they hadn't been of use to the community. They try to move away and feel different when they can read and write. (89)

Sometimes I'd hear how those teachers taught and what education was like in the villages. They said that the arrival of the Spaniards was a conquest, a victory, while we knew in practice that it was just the opposite. . . . This taught me that even though a person may learn to read and write, he should not accept the false education they give our people. Our people must not think as the authorities think. (169–70)

This is why Indians are thought to be stupid. They can't think, they don't know anything, they say. But we have hidden our identity because we needed to resist, we wanted to protect what governments have wanted to take away from us. They have tried to take our things away and impose others on us, be it through religion, through dividing up the land, through schools, through books, through radio, through all things modern. (170–71)

When teachers come into the villages, they bring with them the ideas of capitalism and getting on in life. They try and impose these ideas on us. I remember that in my village there were two teachers for a while and they began teaching the people, but the children told their parents everything they were being taught at school and the parents said: "We don't want our children to become like *ladinos*." And they made the teachers leave. . . . For the Indian, it is better not to study than to become like *ladinos*. (205)

One aspect of the genealogy of Menchú's position expressed here involves the Spanish practice during the Conquest of segregating the children of the Indian aristocracy from their families in order to teach them literacy and Christian doctrine. Walter Mignolo has observed that this practice

> shows that literacy is not instilled without violence. The violence, however, is not located in the fact that the youngsters have been assembled and enclosed day and night. It comes, rather, from the interdiction of having conversations with their parents, particularly with their mothers. In a primary oral society, in which virtually all knowledge is transmitted by means of conversation, the preservation of oral contact was contradictory with the effort to teach how to read and write. Forbidding conversations with the mother meant, basically, depriving the children of the living culture imbedded in the language and preserved and transmitted in speech.[11]

But it is not that, coming from a predominantly oral culture, Menchú does not value literacy or formal education at all. Part of the oedipal struggle with her father recounted in her story involves precisely her desire and eventual success as a teenager at learning first to memorize, then read, passages from the Bible in order to become a Catholic lay catechist (just as later she would learn Spanish and several other Indian languages because of the exigencies of her work as a peasant organizer, and would lead a fight to have a school built in her community). It is rather, as these passages suggest, that she does not accept literacy and book learning, or the narrative of cultural and linguistic modernization that they entail, as either adequate or *normative* cultural modes. She is conscious, among other things, of the holistic relation between the individualization produced by the government schools and the attempts to impose on her community an agrarian reform based on private ownership of parcels (as opposed to its pre-Columbian tradition of communal ownership and sharing of resources). That is why she remains a testimonial narrator rather than an "author"—a subject position that would imply, as in the case of Richard Rodriguez's *Hunger of Memory*, a self-imposed separation from her community and culture of birth (and a loss or change of name). As Doris Sommer has shown, even in the

act of addressing us through the literary artifice of the testimonio—which is built on the convention of truth telling
and openness—Menchú is also withholding information
from us, ostensibly on the grounds that it could be used
against her and her people by academically trained or advised counterinsurgency specialists. She is aware, in other
words, of something we may have forgotten since the Vietnam War: the complicity of the university in cultural (and
sometimes actual) genocide. The concluding words of her
testimonio are indicative of this concern: "I'm still keeping
secret what I think no one should know. Not even anthropologists or intellectuals, no matter how many books they
have, can find out all our secrets" (247).[12]

I suggested in chapter 4 that Menchú's descriptions of the
torture and murder of her brother and mother by the
Guatemalan army represented a kind of testimonial "magic
realism" because of their intensity of detail and affect. I have
been criticized on this point[13] for seeming, from the privileged position of the first world literary intellectual, to aestheticize something that more properly should be dealt with
as an ethical, legal, and political matter. But it is not clear
that these two things—how Menchú works as a narrator
and the implications for solidarity practice of the reception of her narrative—can be separated. Menchú, after all,
does not construct her narrative only from an oral, "non-
Western" model of storytelling but also from her experience
as a lay catechist (which involves the Book of books of Western culture, so to speak), whose function is to dramatize and
allegorize the biblical stories she narrates in order to provoke discussion among the congregation about their contemporary relevance. To recall the Aristotelian distinction
between history and poetry, *I, Rigoberta Menchú* is not just
history in the sense of a chronology of particulars; it also aspires to be *exemplary* in its specificity: "My story is the story
of all poor Guatemalans. My personal experience is the reality of a whole people." Yet against the traditional dichotomy
of logos and body, universal and particular, something of
the experience of the body itself inheres in testimonio. In her
harrowing descriptions of torture and brutality, Menchú is
trying to enact for the reader the force of the genocidal violence that destroyed not only members of her immediate

family but whole communities of her people. By the same token, her evocation of Mayan community life and traditions, which some anthropologists have found idealized and unrepresentative of the real conditions of life and consciousness of contemporary Guatemalan Indians,[14] must be seen, like any ideological project, as in part realistic, in part heuristic or utopian. Her testimonio represents an "ascribed" or possible consciousness, which seeks to interpellate around the communal values that it celebrates a broad movement of Indian and peasant resistance and an international solidarity network to support it.

It would be yet another version of the "native informant" of classical anthropology to grant testimonial narrators like Rigoberta Menchú only the possibility of being "witnesses" (for the prosecution or the defense), and not that of constructing narratives with their own epic or historical authority. That would be a way of saying that the subaltern can of course speak, but only through the institutionally sanctioned authority—itself dependent on and implicated in colonialism and imperialism—of the journalist or ethnographer, who alone has the power to decide what counts in the narrator's "raw material" and to turn it into literature (or "evidence").

To repeat a point I made in chapter 1, Rigoberta Menchú *uses* the testimonio as a form of literature without subscribing to a humanist ideology of the literary, or, what amounts to the same thing, without abandoning her identity and role as an Indian activist to become a professional writer. Testimonio is located at the intersection of the cultural forms of bourgeois humanism—like literature, literary criticism, and theory—which are engendered by, and which sustain, practices of colonial and imperialist domination, and those subaltern cultural practices, both traditional and new, that often constitute testimonio's narrative-descriptive content. It interpellates us in a double register, flattering but also challenging the privatized ethical humanism which is our practical ideology as academics and literati.

The aversion or ambivalence of the testimonio toward literature suggests that cultural democratization must involve not only changes in what counts as literature, but also that literature itself (along with the concomitant standards and practice of "good writing") may in the process lose its centrality and authority as a cultural practice. Where literature in Latin America has been (mainly) a vehicle for engendering an adult, white, male, patriarchal, "lettered" subject, testimonio allows for the emergence—albeit mediated—of subaltern female, gay, indigenous, proletarian, and other identities. But can (or should) these identities be contained within literature?

Let me recall the critical moment in the preface to *I, Rigoberta Menchú* where Elisabeth Burgos-Debray debates with herself about what to correct in the transcription of the recordings of Menchú's conversations with her. One might object that the interlocutor is manipulating the material the informant provides to suit her own cosmopolitan political, intellectual, and aesthetic predilections were it not for the fact this is not something Menchú herself would have resisted or resented, since her point in telling her story to Burgos-Debray was precisely to make it available to reading publics both in Guatemala and abroad. For what has happened between Menchú's speech and Burgos-Debray's preface is that her narrative has become both a "text" and "literary." There is perhaps no more mediated and editorially mutilated testimonial text in Latin American literature than the *Autobiography* of the Cuban ex-slave Juan Francisco Manzano, which was prepared in 1835 at the urging of the Cuban liberal Domingo Del Monte, corrected and edited by the overtly abolitionist novelist Anselmo Suárez y Romero, and subsequently abridged and translated for a metropolitan audience by the major agent of British imperialism in Cuba, Richard Madden (the original for the character Marlon Brando played in Pontecorvo's *Burn*). Sylvia Molloy has compared the unedited version of Manzano's original, handwritten manuscript with the published versions in Spanish and English. She concludes that

> the *Autobiografía* as Manzano wrote it, with its run-on sentences, breathless paragraphs, dislocated syntax and idiosyncratic misspellings, vividly portrays that quandary—an anxiety of origins, ever renewed, that provides the text with the stubborn, uncontrolled energy that is possibly its major achievement. The writing, *in itself*, is the best self-portrait we have of Manzano, his greatest contribution to literature; at the

same time, it is what translators, editors and critics cannot tolerate . . . [The] notion (shared by many) that there is a clear narrative imprisoned, as it were, in Manzano's *Autobiografía*, waiting for the hand of the cultivated editor to free it fom the slag—this notion that the impure text must be replaced by a clean (white?) version of it to be readable—amounts to another, aggressive mutilation, that of denying the text readability in its own terms.[15]

Can we take this, mutatis mutandis, as an allegory of both the production of testimonio and its incorporation into the humanities? What was at stake in the Stanford debate was the opposition of two different reading lists—one traditional and Euro- and phallocentric ("dead white males"), the other third worldist and feminist.[16] But literature and the humanities as such—not to speak of Stanford's role in the formation and reproduction of class power in the United States and in the global economy—were never put into question. They were, rather, the condition of possibility of struggle over the curriculum and the reading lists in the first place. I understand this position, and it is one I pursue in my own work of presenting and interpreting texts in the classroom (which has included teaching courses on Central American revolutionary literature at, among other places, Stanford).

But in dealing with testimonio, I have also begun to discover in myself a kind of posthumanist agnosticism about literature. In spite of Ernesto Laclau's point—which I consider extremely important in other contexts—that ideological signifiers do not have a necessary "class-belonging," the problem of testimonio indicates that literature cannot be simply appropriated by this or that social project. It is deeply marked by its own historical and institutional entanglements, its "tradition of service," so to speak. There may come a time when we have a new community of things we can call literature; but not yet. Among the many lessons testimonio has to offer is one that suggests that it is no longer a question of "reading against the grain," as in the various academic practices of textual deconstruction with which we are familiar, but of beginning to read against literature itself.

Part III
After Literature

CHAPTER 6

The Politics of Latin American Postmodernism

In part II, I made the case that testimonio implies a challenge to the loss of the authority of orality in the context of processes of cultural modernization that privilege literacy, writing, and literature as norms of expression. What is phallic—in the Lacanian sense—about the institution of literature is the need for it to be engendered by an authorizing signifier of inscription (which gives "permission to write"). If this is so, then it is not clear what is accomplished by shifting that signifier to some part of women's anatomy (or experience). The persistence of orality (in women's culture, in the culture of colonized and/or proletarianized subjects) should be seen as a *conscious and active* resistance to writing and literacy, not just as an effect of gender difference and discrimination that can be overcome by "taking up the pen," so to speak.

The montage of the four different modes of narration that make up the text of *Alabi's World*, Richard Price's intricate reconstruction of the social history of the Dutch slave colony of Suriname in the eighteenth century—oral stories and legends of the runaway slaves; administrative reports by the colonial authorities; diaries of missionaries; and the historian's own mediating discourse—also enacts the different forms of racial and class conflict in that society and, in turn, their discursive forms of cultural legitimation and agency. The modes of narration, the way actors invest happenings with historical or symbolic meaning, are also markers of social practice. In a similar way, testimonios like *I, Rigoberta Menchú* are, as we have seen, not only *representations* but also a *means* of subaltern resistance.

The populist critique of modernism in Latin American literature tends to set up a dichotomy between complex, antirepresentational, value-leveling, high-culture forms of literature of the sort represented by Boom narrative and simple, lineal, representational, value-affirming, "popular" narrative forms like the testimonio. The first are seen as "imported" or imposed from above, and thus as complicit with imperialism and neocolonialism, the second as the more or less spontaneous expression of "the people" in conditions of underdevelopment and exploitation. That some of the force of that dichotomy has crept into my own thinking about testimonio is evident from the essays in part II. But while testimonio clearly situates itself against modernist literary models that are based on a subversion or rejection of narratives of identity, it is not an autonomous or "authentic" form of subaltern culture (it would be difficult to imagine what that might be, since the subaltern is in any case a *relational* identity). As in the argument more familiarly made for postmodernist art generally, its power of agency depends on its ability to function in the historically and socially constituted space that separates "high" and "low" cultures in Latin America. Whatever its initial connection to a world of primary orality, it comes to us as a "text," and the nature of any text—for example, the perceived qualities of testimonial as opposed to Boom narrative—is determined by its place in an already constituted discourse system. Rather than a clear dichotomy between an "oral" popular culture of resistance and a "written" colonial and/or neocolonial high culture, then, testimonio involves a series of negotiations between different subject positions and their legitimizing discourses. This is implicit in its very situation of enunciation, which confronts radically the subject positions of the emitter and the receiver. But the negotiation can also occur on either side of this relationship (Menchú has to struggle through her own ambivalent relation to Spanish-language literacy; in constructing her story, she depends partly on the model of biblical narrative that she learned as a lay catechist; her eventual identity as a narrator is hardly a "traditional" one; there are no "pure" Indian languages not modified by colonialism).

Testimonio is no more capable of transcending the oppositions it entails (elite/subaltern, literature/oral narrative, metropolitan/creole, *ladino*/Indian, white/mestizo or black, urban/rural, intellectual/manual work) than more purely "literary" forms of writing or narrative: that would require social and cultural transformations capable of initiating literacy campaigns and developing the educational and economic infrastructures necessary to create and sustain radically democratized reading publics that have as a prior condition the victory of revolutionary movements. But, as we have seen, it does represent a new way of articulating these oppositions, and thus of defining new paradigms for the relationship between the intelligentsia and the popular classes, and a new sense of the "national" based on heterogeneity rather than mastery.

Paradoxically, and against the expectations of its original protagonists, however, testimonio does not seem particularly well suited to become the primary narrative form of periods of postrevolutionary consolidation, as in Cuba after the sixties or Nicaragua after the early eighties, perhaps because its very dynamics depend on the conditions of acute social and cultural inequality that fuel the revolutionary impulse in the first place.[1] Like its ancestor, the picaresque novel, testimonio is a *transitional* cultural form appropriate to processes of social upheaval, but also destined to give way to different forms of representation as these processes move to other stages and the human collectivities that are their agents come into possession of (or lose) new forms of power and knowledge.

But this transitional character of testimonio is perhaps also another sign of its relationship with the more general problematic of postmodernism, to which I now turn.

George Yúdice asks the inevitable question: "Can one speak of postmodernism in Latin America?"[2] The very idea makes one think of that condition of colonial or neocolonial dependency in which goods that have become shopworn or out of fashion in the metropolis are, like the marvels of the gypsies in *One Hundred Years of Solitude* or the Baroque, exported to the periphery, where they enjoy a profitable second life. For, after all the articles, books, conferences, and media hype, after Lyotard and Habermas, Jean Baudrillard and Pee-wee

Herman, Soho painters and "new social movements" à la Mouffe and Laclau, surely the concept of postmodernism has itself begun to be devoured by habitualization and to lose the power of aesthetic *ostranenie* that recommended it to our attention in the first place. Yet it is precisely at this point that it has come in the last three or four years to the top of the agenda of Latin American literary and cultural discussion.[3]

There are a number of good reasons to answer Yúdice's question in the negative. To begin with, what does it mean to call "postmodern" social formations that have not yet gone through the stage of modernity, or, perhaps more to the point, that display what is sometimes called an "uneven modernity"? (What society does not, however?) To compound the problem, *modernismo* and *postmodernismo* designate, in Latin American Spanish, early twentieth-century literary movements that have no direct correspondence to what is understood as modernism and postmodernism in English (the not quite identical Spanish equivalent of modernism is *vanguardismo*, not *modernismo*). Speaking from the left, Nelson Osorio has argued that postmodernism, like liberalism, is yet another imported *grand récit* that does not fit a Latin American reality that needs to produce its own forms of cultural periodization, and he has been echoed in this claim, from the other side of the political spectrum, by Octavio Paz, whose position on postmodernism is akin to that of Hilton Kramer and the *New Criterion* in the United States.[4]

Clearly also, as in the association of the Baroque with the Counter-Reformation that we explored earlier, there is a coincidence between the appearance of postmodernism and the global hegemony of the New Right after 1979, and between cultural phenomena identified as postmodernist— U.S. architecture, media, popular music, and fashion, for example—and the present sensibility and strategies of transnational capitalism, a coincidence that gives some credence to the idea that postmodernism is a new form of cultural imperialism (in Andreas Huyssen's image, "the American International"). There is the related danger that—as in the case of Baudrillard's books on the United States—the production of a postmodernist "sublime" in relation to Latin America may involve the aesthetic festishization of its social, cultural, and economic status quo (as abject, chaotic, heterogeneous, carnivalesque, etc.), thereby attenuating the urgency for radical social change and displacing it into cultural dilettantism and quietism.[5] Finally, there is Neil Larsen's skeptical warning—I will return to it later—that even where there is a "promise of subversion" in postmodernism, this "seems no more and no less genuine than that long-ago discredited pledge of the modernist vanguard to, as it were, seize hold of capital's cultural and psychic mechanisms without firing a shot."[6]

But these reservations also seem to miss or mistake something of the nature of postmodernism itself, which is bound up precisely with the dynamics of interaction between local cultures and an instantaneous and omnipresent global culture. In Fredric Jameson's influential, if much-contested, rendering (now itself globally disseminated), postmodernism in its most general sense is a periodizing concept whose function is to correlate the emergence of new formal features in culture with the technological, economic, and social features of this new, transnational stage of capitalism, which is now beginning to envelop even the formerly semiautarkic space of the Communist bloc countries.[7]

Jameson's by now familiar argument is that there is no longer an "outside"—nature, the Third World, the psyche, T. S. Eliot's Great Tradition, the high modernist artwork— from which to observe or resist the system. It is not that, say, *Terminator 2* or *Thelma and Louise* play in Havana or Buenos Aires *after* their New York-Hollywood run, as a dependency-theory approach to cultural transmission (of the sort implicit in Mattelart and Dorfman's classic *How to Read Donald Duck*) would hold. In the mode of postmodernism, the Hollywood blockbusters open everywhere more or less simultaneously (the slight lag in the case of Havana being due, paradoxically, to the fact that since the blockade limits the Cubans' ability to buy U.S. media material directly, they have to make pirated copies of it—a process they call *fusilar*, shooting). Moreover, as I noted in chapter 1, the notion of a differential appropriation of international mass culture, which was a mainstay of anti-imperialist cultural and media studies in the past, is precisely something that postmodernist reception theory puts into question.

It may be that Jameson's totalizing construction of postmodernism involves, as Aijaz Ahmad has argued, "a suppression of the multiplicity of significant difference among and within both the advanced capitalist countries and the imperialised formations."[8] Globalization of capital and communications does not mean homogenization; if anything, it tends to aggravate the normal capitalist dynamics of combined and uneven development, producing, as in the earlier moment of Lenin's *Imperialism*, the welter of conflicting national, ethnic, and regional particularisms that is the stuff of the daily international news. On the other hand, phenomena that in the past might have represented the cultural authenticity of national liberation struggles—for example, the decision of the Kenyan novelist Ngugi to write only in his tribal language, Kikuyu; or the guerrilla testimonio; or the Pan-Caribbean cultural politics of Cuba's Casa de las Américas; or South African township jive music; or Mahasweta Devi's Bengali stories; or the contemporary filipino film *Perfumed Nightmare*—may be seen today as "postmodern" in some sense or other, even in the very heterogeneity and specificity of their aesthetic-ideological strategies. The (postcolonial) "margin is at the center" not because of any formal logic of supplementarity (nor even less because it has taken over the center) but because it is in the process of being drawn very deeply and rapidly into global economic and cultural networks. It is no accident that the decentered subject of poststructuralist theory is also more often than not "cheap labor" these days, in both an increasingly industrialized Third World and (with corresponding deindustrialization) the advanced capitalist democracies and the former Communist bloc. It follows, for Jameson, that the choice is not between postmodernism and something that is clearly other than it, but rather between the different ideological "spins" that can be given to postmodernist culture, what he calls an "aesthetics of cognitive mapping": "The point is that we are *within* the culture of postmodernism to the point where its facile repudiation is as impossible as any equally facile celebration of it is complacent and corrupt."[9]

From this perspective, which I share, the importance of the postmodernism debate in Latin America has to do above all with its implication in the process of revision (or replacement) of the discourse of the Latin American left in the wake of the defeat of both the armed-struggle strategy represented by guerrilla *foquismo* and the "peaceful road to socialism" represented by Allende's coalition-building electoral politics (and the more recent problematization of Cuba as a model for an achieved socialist society). In a context in which the argument for postmodernism in Latin American literary and cultural criticism was—initially—being made mainly from anti- (or post-) Marxist positions, and in which a visceral anti-postmodernism has been dominant on the left,[10] it seemed important to try to offer a vision of postmodern aesthetics that not only emphasized its affinity with the political project of the left but also saw it as an important means of renovating its exhausted or discredited political imaginary.

Something like the activities of the Salvadoran artists and writers working in tandem with the FMLN may seem quite distant from the concerns of the New York "performance artists" profiled in the trendy and affluent pages of Andy Warhol's *Interview*. But the U.S. postmodernists are also clearly the generational equivalent—Godard's "children of Marx and Coca-Cola"—of the cultural fellow travelers of the Central American revolutionary movements represented by groups like Frente Ventana in Nicaragua or ASTAC (Asociación Salvadoreña de Trabajadores en Arte y Cultura) in El Salvador (and, like them, are under attack from the right). Is the new Central American left cultural production a response to dependency generally and thus in particular to postmodernism as the current "cultural dominant" ("good," politically correct third world as opposed to "bad," narcissistic first world stuff); or is it itself a form of postmodernist—or "postmodern," since these terms are not exactly synonymous—culture? Such an indeterminacy reflects the debate about the ideological valence of the term in the United States and Western Europe.[11]

Let me use George Yúdice's 1985 essay, "Central American Testimonio," to argue the negative view, with the understanding that it is a particular kind of postmodernism that he is concerned with—one closely identified with avant-garde positions in art and philosophy like Kristeva's—and that his own position in fact favors what has come to be known as a "postmodernism of resistance."[12] "First world postmodernism," Yúdice writes, "feeds off and is at the expense of an occluded third world warrant." The inclination, which he attributes initially to Octavio Paz, to identify Latin American Boom literature and culture with postmodernism, "supposedly because it is decentered, fragmented, carnivalesque, unrepresentable, marginal . . . is a ruse which facilitates greater material-symbolic penetration and colonization by transnational logic." Yúdice's case is rather for "the viability of the counterhegemonic projects of popular culture" directed against local capitalist and oligarchic domination and transnational cultural penetration. By the early 1970s, Latin American literature had broken with the canon of the Boom and "splintered into various trends—realist, nationalist, regionalist, historical, testimonial, feminist, ethnic—which bespeak a break with the drama of the highly individualized subject of modernist culture and a turn toward a new collective subject living through the individual or multiple voices of the text (writer, narrator, witness, character, persona)." This decentering of the subject is also a feature of first world postmodernist *écriture*—in its refusal of representation and its cultivation of the "abject" or "hyperreal" (Kristeva, Didion's book on El Salvador)—but in a way that facilitates breaking down traditional cultural patterns and values in the service of reorganization of societies and concepts of selfhood proposed by transnational capitalism.

Yúdice draws in particular on Néstor García Canclini's questioning of the teleological imperative of capitalism—the sense that it is destined to create a homogeneous world system—and his concomitant revalorization of local popular cultures, which Canclini sees as constituted by a process of unequal appropriation of both economic and cultural capital by subaltern groups and by the transformation of their general and specific conditions of family and community life and work. "The flux of capitalism schizo-advocates like Deleuze and Guattari celebrate as liberational is an even greater form of oppression for Third World peoples," Yúdice suggests. Unlike colonialism, it does not "extinguish their cultures but rather restructures and resemioticizes them." The popular or subaltern sectors struggle against this process, "resignifying their patterns of production and consumption, ethnic customs, culinary and religious practices, sexual relations, etc." Cultural forms and traditions in Latin America are destabilized and/or overrun by centrifugal currents deriving from the metropolis, including the tremendous expansion of the mass media, but cultural despoliation is never complete, and new cultural forms emerge that resist, neutralize, or co-opt the forces of terror, abjection, and deterritorialization.

In the field of literature, Yúdice argues, these new forms involve the kinds of poetry and narrative that emerged in connection with the Central American revolutionary movements. Although, from a metropolitan perspective, postmodernism is identified with Latin American Boom narrative of the sixties,[13] this new literature, particularly in its testimonial forms, draws its inspiration and forms not from a previous literary or artistic avant-garde but from the spread of popular struggles themselves and from the new forms of mobilization and discourse associated with liberation theology:

> During the 60s social changes were taking place, such as Paolo Freire's conscientization literacy movement, the formation of Christian Base Communities and peasant and worker organizations, which were totally absent from the canonical texts of the literary "boom." The "popular" was either essentialized in petit bourgeois recreations of peasant and indigenous speech and culture (e.g., Salarrué in El Salvador, Asturias in Guatemala), or pawned off as mass culture (Fuentes, Puig, Sarduy). . . . Like the Christian Base Communities, which are grassroots movements in which popular (i.e., exploited) sectors reread the gospel as the "good news" of the coming of the Kingdom of God here on earth, the testimonial emphasizes a rereading of culture as lived history and a profession of faith in the struggles of the oppressed.

Unlike first world postmodernist *écriture* and poststructuralism—which depend on the denial or deconstruction of representation—forms like the testimonio embody a "counterhegemonic project of representation, identification, solidarity, affect, and resistance to transnational penetration of culture." Thus, Yúdice concludes, "the postmodernism which Jameson understands as culturally dominant is precisely what is put into question by these contestatory discourses."

Yúdice's argument, then, is for a posthumanist and anti-modernist, but also anti-postmodernist, cultural production in Latin America. But by its own situational logic—which privileges orality, testimonio, subjectivity, feminism, non-instrumental rationality, popular culture, the local, the sub-altern—the argument could lead to the alternative conclusion that the new forms of popular-democratic cultural resistance in Latin America he champions also rise up on a postmodern terrain.[14]

Such a move involves shifting or redefining the concept of postmodernism in Latin America in a strategic way. For Jameson, postmodernism is essentially a first world phenomenon—the crisis and mutation of the forms of ideological legitimation of advanced capitalist consumer societies, or postfordism—whose third world correlate is Boom narrative with its strategies of transculturation, hybridization, and so on. But, as Roberto González Echevarría noted some time ago, the identification of postmodernism and the Boom is in fact asymmetrical. Since part of the aesthetic ideology of postmodernism is precisely to question notions like "great author" and "great novel," which are decisive for Boom ideology, the moment of postmodernism in Latin American writing is more that of what gets called the *postboom* or *los novísimos*—that is, the new writers and literary production that emerge after the crisis year of 1973, which marks the end of the sixties and the increasing power of the right in both Latin America and the United States. In this sense (and it is one that Yúdice shares), Puig, Nicaraguan workshop poetry, and testimonio are postmodern, but Paz, Cortázar, Fuentes, and Vargas Llosa are not; rather, they and their colleagues represent the Latin American equivalent of Anglo-European high modernism.

The three interrelated problematics that are usually taken as defining postmodernism are: (1) the collapse of the distinction between elite and popular (or mass) cultures, sometimes expressed as the loss of aesthetic autonomy (a collapse that carries with it what Jameson calls in his postmodernism

essay "a prodigious expansion of culture throughout the social realm, to the point at which everything in our social
life—from economic value and state power to practices and
to the very structure of the psyche itself—can be said to
have become 'cultural' in some original and as yet untheorized sense" (*Postmodernism*, 48); (2) the end of the "great
narratives" of Western progress and enlightenment with
which the specifically aesthetic projects of first realist and
then modernist art were associated; and (3) the crisis (or
"death") of the subject.[15] Although postmodernism is clearly
related to the rampant commodification and reorganization
of even high culture in advanced capitalist societies, at the
same time, as Benjamin anticipated, the loss of aura or desublimation of the artwork that such a commodification portends offers the possibility of very radical forms of cultural
democratization. Postmodernism is not only, as Lyotard
suggests, an elite form of aesthetic populism (abandoning,
in the manner of Vargas Llosa or the U.S. minimalist com-
posers like Philip Glass, experimentalism in favor of "pleas-
ing the public"); it has involved in both cultural production
and consumption women, and lower-middle-class, working-
class, and minority sectors of the population previously excluded in general from (and by) bourgeois high culture
forms like literature. An obvious example is the creative energy and labor represented by rock and rock-influenced
third world musics like reggae, which both derive from and
address proletarian and popular milieus.

In these terms, the aesthetic and political significance of
something like testimonio or Cardenal's workshop poetry
project in Nicaragua depended on their ability to (1) function
in the historically constituted space that separates elite and
popular cultures in the region; (2) generate new postcolonial, non-Eurocentric narratives of regional historical-cultural
identity; and (3) provide new forms of subject identification
of the personal-in-the-collective. To the extent that Central
American artists or writers were involved with traditional
left parties or sects in the region, they were concerned with
redefining (or, in the case of Nicaragua, creating) an inherited Marxist (in both Leninist and social-democratic senses)
metanarrative of progress and modernization—what Gayatri Spivak calls "the mode of production narrative"—to fit

the very different modalities of their regional and national histories.[16]

If postmodernism is understood not as a more or less coherent cultural period or style like Romanticism or modernism itself, but rather (this is Yúdice's own redefinition) as "multiple local aesthetic-ideological responses/proposals in the face of, against, and within transnationalization" ("múltiples respuestas/propuestas estético-ideológicas locales ante, frente y dentro de la transnacionalización") (Yúdice 1989, 108), then the condition of new forms of cultural production involved in the Central American revolutionary movements is coincident with first world postmodernism, rather than its other.[17]

Of course, if that is the case, then the defeat of the Sandinistas in the February 1990 elections might strike a cautionary note about the validity of such a "cultural" politics. This I take to be the point of Neil Larsen's essay "Postmodernism and Imperialism: Theory and Politics in Latin America."[18] Against the usual dismissal of postmodernism as a pernicious and reactionary metropolitan imposition, Larsen grants that there is something like what he calls a Latin American "left postmodernism," which he finds exemplified in the "ethic of survival" represented by Rigoberta Menchú's testimonio, Enrique Dussel's analectics and liberation theology generally, Ernesto Laclau's work on populism, and Roberto Fernández Retamar's celebration—in *Caliban* and elsewhere—of Latin American alterity.[19]

Despite their starting point in the historical reality of combined and unequal development, however, Larsen feels that the left postmodernists "all, to one degree or another, proceed to distort this reality into a new irrationalist and spontaneist myth. Marginality is postulated as the condition which, purely by virtue of its objective *situation*, spontaneously gives rise to the *subversive particularity* upon which postmodern politics pins its hopes"(6). "The strategic watchword seems to be 'hegemony' . . . [which] implies a need to substitute a form of organization based on spontaneously arising social and cultural ideologies and practices for an 'older' one of party-based, consciousness-raising agitation and recruitment" (7).

These "politics of spontaneism," Larsen concludes, are "the derivative *effects* of retrograde developments within the left itself, of what amounts to the *conscious political* decision to give up the principle of revolution as a scientifically grounded activity, as a praxis with a rational foundation." Such a decision "rests on an intellectual distrust of the masses, a view of the masses as beyond the reach of reason and hence to be guided by myth" (9). I am putting words in his mouth, but I assume that it follows by implication for Larsen that Sandinism, as an example of a political articulation built around a quasi-mythic sense of the national-popular (the signifier of Sandino himself) and lacking both a coherent "line" and, because of its polyclass nature, an unambiguous base in a conscious, organized working class, is unable to sustain its transformative project and its own strategic coherence in the face of U.S. aggression and the burgeoning class struggle within Nicaragua itself after 1979.

As an "eloquent refutation" of this sort of politics, Larsen offers an episode from one of the key narratives of Central American revolutionary militancy, Roque Dalton's testimonio of the life of one of the founders of the Salvadoran Communist party, *Miguel Mármol*. Mármol describes how, sent to organize a union of rural workers in 1930 in his hometown of Ilopango, he overcomes their hostility and distrust, motivated in part by their suspicion that he is antireligious. Larsen cites in particular a passage where Mármol recalls that "as the people began to talk about working conditions, it wasn't hard to hear, over and over again, concepts that sounded to me just like the 'class struggle,' the 'dictatorship of the proletariat,' etc."[20] Mármol's task, he concludes (offering this as a model for the practice of the contemporary left), is "not that of 'enlightening' the 'backward' masses, nor is it simply to acknowledge 'what the people thought' as sovereign. Rather, it is to collect these isolated concepts, to *articulate* them, and to draw the logically necessary conclusions."

I am not sure a "politics of spontaneism" (an older left discourse would have spoken also of "voluntarism") is the necessary consequence of the notion of ideological interpellation advanced by Althusser and his followers (compare, for example, Larsen's characterization with the account of popular-democratic interpellation in Laclau's essay on populism).[21] Nearer at hand, though, Larsen seems to overlook an important feature of the textual dynamics of *Miguel Mármol* itself. For this text, like most testimonios, is founded not only on the direct discourse of the narrator, which is historical and narrative, but also on the relation between that narrator and the interlocutor—that is, Roque Dalton himself—who stands in for the *contemporary* political subject who is being interpellated by the narrative. In Mármol's remark about "concepts that sounded to me just like," the point for Dalton is surely that the concepts were *not literally* "class struggle" or "dictatorship of the proletariat"—that is, those of a standard, Eurocentric, Marxist discourse ("proletariat" is a Latin neologism; "dictatorship" is the form of government the Salvadoran people have experienced for most of their history; where owners are mainly European and workers mainly indigenous or mestizo, "class struggle" itself can be experienced as a racial-cultural matter).

But even with this revision Dalton is clearly *not* proposing the Salvadoran Communist party of the thirties or the abortive uprising of 1932 led by Farabundo Martí (both products of the ultrasectarian "Third Period" of the Comintern, which coincided with Stalin's rise to power and forced collectivization in the Soviet Union) as a model for revolutionary activism in the present. Mármol, Dalton notes in his introduction, is "the prototypical incarnation of the Latin American communist worker and peasant leader of what is usually called 'the classical period,' 'the heroic era,' of the parties that, as sections of the Communist International, sprang up and developed in nearly every country on the continent" (27–28). Dalton's own perspective, by contrast, is that of a generation that comes to maturity in the wake of de-Stalinization, the Cuban Revolution as a new model of revolutionary agency in the Americas, and the international New Left of the sixties. During the years *Miguel Mármol* was being prepared (1966–71), the Salvadoran Communist party, to which both men belonged, itself split over the issue of armed struggle, with Dalton leaving in 1969 to throw in his lot with the Guevarist and left-Christian ERP, then in formation. The conflict between the two men—which also straddles the problem of the relation of the intelligentsia to the working class and peasantry—is played out at the level of the composition of the text itself: Dalton, who was educated to be a lawyer, notes his "natural tendency to complicate things, which bristles seriously at Mármol's tendency to simplify them." Despite their differences, however, Dalton declares that "more than to argue with Mármol, I feel my duty as a Central American revolutionary is to assume him; just as we assume, in order to see the face of the future, our terrible national history" (23). At the same time, he makes explicit his own priorities, which favor a different strategy than Mármol. The point of the testimonio is not, then, as Larsen supposes, to provide a clear normative model of revolutionary activism and organization, but rather to enact, in the representation of one "of the elements of democratic culture produced by the exploited strata and classes within the 'national culture' in general" (28), a dialogical confrontation of differing left traditions and strategic perspectives in a way that Dalton thought might be useful for the development of the Salvadoran left in the decade of the seventies and beyond.

Could we not describe Dalton's strategy in *Miguel Mármol* as a variant of the postmodernist genre of what Linda Hutcheon has called historiographic metafiction?[22] Does the question seem inappropriate because it subsumes a Latin American cultural phenomenon under a North American one; or because in the United States such fictions (Barth, DeLillo, Doctorow, Alice Walker, etc.) are "just literature," with hazy ideological effects somewhere in the psychic distance, whereas Dalton was on the front line of the ideological recomposition of the left in El Salvador in a period of tremendous crisis and repression, indeed paid for his beliefs with his life?

But to make a distinction of this sort between literature and "real" politics is, of course, precisely to ignore the effects of the collapse of the autonomy of culture that postmodernist theory both diagnoses, I think correctly, and celebrates—effects that, on the other hand, are easy to see (and lament) when it is a question of MTV commodity aesthetics.

What Larsen's critique of postmodernism betrays (and what it shares with a social-democratic counterpart like Habermas's) is both the discomfort of what Gramsci called the "traditional intellectual" or aesthete in the face of the emergence of mass culture and the corresponding nostalgia for a rational politics of clearly defined class-based parties, based on the assumption of a transparency of representation between class position, self-consciousness as a historical agent, party, and strategic line. The possibility of such a transparency was what the Lukács of *History and Class Consciousness* in the twenties termed the "ascribed consciousness" of a class (that is, the consciousness that a class *should* have, given its position in the relations of production, rather than its actual or empirically observable consciousness).

But this is surely a transparency seriously put into question by not only a culturalist or poststructuralist emphasis on the relative autonomy of the political, but even a modest appreciation of the reality of the unconscious in human life. It is not to denigrate the enlightenment of the masses, as Larsen supposes, that a postmodern position emphasizes subjectivity and cultural relativity; it is to underline the fact that intellectuals and political organizers are themselves constructed as subjects in the field of desire, and that a politics that does not pass the test of this field will fail.

What is at stake in postmodernism is a new conception of cultural and aesthetic agency that implies something like an inversion of Walter Benjamin's slogan, at the end of "The Work of Art in the Age of Mechanical Reproduction," that while fascism seeks to aestheticize politics, communism politicizes art. From a postmodernist perspective, not only does the left need to aestheticize politics, it needs to make of aesthetic experience itself—cultural creation and consumption—one of the forms of agency of postcapitalist social life (Larsen's *Modernism and Hegemony*, by contrast, bears the subtitle *A Materialist Critique of Aesthetic Agencies*). Such a shift involves accepting the challenge of mass culture and the mass media—rather than simply dismissing these, as has been the case in the dominant models of Latin American media criticism—as sites for the production of false consciousness.[23] It also involves critiquing the ways in which the left in its previous incarnations was, in its own cultural ideologies, implicated with a university-based, essentially Eurocentric literary humanism and, since the thirties in particular, with aesthetic modernism in the English-language sense of the term—a relation that empowered but also limited its political reach and effectiveness.[24]

Postmodernity implies that the left can no longer construct its opposition to capitalism in the name of a universal telos of secularization and modernization: the crisis of the statist model of actually existing socialism is testimony to the fact that, as Stanley Aronowitz puts it, "as a modernizing strategy, socialism fails in an international economy dominated by capitalist commodity relations." What replaces this telos are "local" narratives, built around the desire for democratization, social justice, the defense and expansion of personal rights, identity politics. "The new social movements," Aronowitz notes, "enter the national and international political arena speaking a language of localism and regionalism, a discourse that, although internationalist, does not appeal to class solidarity as its primary line of attack, but addresses power itself as an antagonist."[25]

Larsen is correct to note that what is problematic in the micropolitics of these movements, as in the contingent aesthetic celebration of alterity, marginality, and pastiche, is the lack of any overall strategy for conquering hegemony beyond the sometimes feverish activity of the individual movements or ad hoc "alliance politics," since there is no sense that any issue or contradiction is or can be made central. But while it is clear that such movements need not be explicitly anticapitalist, capitalism, which has a stake in maintaining conditions of subalternity and exploitation of all sorts, represents a limit-condition to their full development. And the force of class struggle itself is not entirely suspended in postmodernist heterology: some of the most powerful of the new social movements are precisely the kinds of union organizations and union-community coalitions that have sprung up in the wake of the effects of the globalization of capital, such as South Africa's COSATU (Confederation of South African Trade Unions) or the Brazilian metal workers' union.[26]

Nor is a postmodernist politics necessarily an "antipolitics" of dispersed single-issue or identity-politics groups (though this is certainly its most characteristic manifestation). Even in defeat (and precisely because of their commitment to implement and respect democratic processes in the face of massive foreign aggression and interference), it seems to me that the Sandinistas are exemplary of the emergence of a postmodern but still explicitly socialist political agency in Latin America; I believe their political project is by no means exhausted. One could also point along these lines to such "national-popular" (in Gramsci's sense of this term) formations as the African National Congress, the FMLN-FDR in El Salvador (which has evolved from being a coalition of Leninist sects to a broad left coalition embracing parties, guerrilla groups, and "people's organizations"), the Brazilian Workers Party, the recent growth of Latin American women's groups and feminist activism, the sort of labor cum ecological activism represented by Chico Mendes, Rigoberta Menchú's CUC (Committee of Campesino Unity) in Guatemala (now destroyed), the left electoral coalition around Cuauhtémoc Cárdenas in Mexico, or even the possible implications of the Rainbow Coalition in the United States.

There is a sense in these movements—which are in effect parties of the left of a new type—of a need to retain within themselves a heterogeneity of new social movements and even of class components (this need is also the source of their internal problems and contradictions, since they have to appease groups whose interests may be structurally incompatible—as the very distinct cases of Solidarity in Poland or the Sandinistas in Nicaragua suggest). Yet, at the same time, they seek to interpellate "the people" as a popular majority around a counterhegemonic project of state power with a coherent social vision and policy guidelines and a set of values to give these legitimacy. Just as the socialist and communist parties of the traditional type have come into crisis, there is no doubt that *a certain* dogmatic, historicist, Eurocentric Marxism has become "post" in Latin America as elsewhere. In the lapidary formulation of Adolfo Sánchez Vázquez (reproduced, strategically, by the Cuban journal *Casa de las Américas*), one continues to have faith in and to struggle for what Habermas calls the "project of modernity" bequeathed by the Enlightenment; but one can only contribute to the establishment, clarification, and leadership of this project of emancipation, which in the conditions of postmodernity continues to be socialism—a postmodern socialism, if you wish—to the extent that one's theory of the reality that has to be transformed and of the possibilities and ways of doing this is attentive to the voices of that reality and frees itself from the teleological, progressivist, productivist, and Eurocentric conceptions of modernity that impregnated even Marx's own thought and have continued in force up to the present day.[27]

At the same time, one must recognize that, because by virtue of postmodernism's very critique of essentialism there is no *necessary* connection between it and the left, a postmodernism of the right (on the model of what Stuart Hall has called Thatcher's "authoritarian populism" in Great Britain) is also flourishing in Latin America, represented inter alia by Fujimori, or his rival Mario Vargas Llosa (both as a novelist and politician), Hernando de Soto's neoliberal economic manifesto *The Other Path*, Menem in Argentina, the complex politics of narcotraffic, or simply Miami. And to indicate that the left must operate on a new terrain in new ways does not, of course, guarantee that it can or will: witness its current impasse in the Southern Cone countries, despite its intimate and decisive participation in the process of redemocratization. Finally, if the problems of the Latin American left are seen from the perspective (which in a Maoist form would be that of Sendero Luminoso in Peru, for example) that there already exists a model of party building and political struggle that simply has not been implemented effectively (because of "bad leadership," opportunism, economism, revisionism, and the like), or that the failure of this or that left strategy was mainly due to the force of U.S. destabilization rather than problems internal to it, then the effort to relate postmodernism and the project of socialism in Latin America should be seen not only as "culturalist" in the worst sense but also as potentially demoralizing and divisive—something like an attempt to "yuppify" left cultural politics.

I would like to conclude on a different note, however, by recalling that the fourth or fifth largest Spanish-speaking country in the world today (and perhaps by the year 2000 the third) is the United States (after Mexico, Spain, Colombia, and Argentina). This fact (of postmodernity) should surely go some way toward deconstructing that binary construction that opposed all classes in the United States as a bloc to Latin America and vice versa. If, as is often said, the question of Latin American postmodernism is ultimately linked to the process of redemocratization, then surely it is significant that by 2076, the tricentennial of the American Revolution, the majority of the population of the United States—assuming it still exists as a single nation-state—will be of African, Hispanic, Native American, or Asian descent. As José Martí anticipated, the center will then be (at) the margin.

The reader will have have noticed that I appear in this chapter to have come full circle from the critique of the literary in the name of the subaltern with which I began this book to a reinvocation, in the shape of the discussion of *Miguel Mármol*, of the literary text as a model for new forms of revolutionary or progressive social agency (the debate with Neil Larsen is over what kind of model). Similarly, my focus on testimonio, which is, after all, a new guest at the table of literature, risks reinscribing literature's traditional status as a master discourse (with the related danger that testimonio may involve, for comfortably located first world intellectuals, the illusion of an ethically and epistemologically privileged access to a third world or subaltern other). As in the United States, postmodernist practice in Latin America has tended to be most compelling in collective theater (*teatro de creación colectiva*), performance, hybrid art/pop song forms, radio- and telenovelas, video, painting and sculpture, *poesía de taller*, and the like. The problem of literature-centered concepts of postmodernism like Linda Hutcheon's is that postmodernism is not only a matter of modifying previous models of literary narrative, but of *depriviteging* literature itself as a dominant cultural mode. This is a particularly potent issue in the Third World where, as we have seen, literature has been implicated in the contradictions and failures of dependent modernization. (Ngugi wa Thiongo's shift from writing in English to writing in Kikuyu, to which I have alluded, was also a shift from the novel as such to more informal and accessible forms of storytelling and theater.)

With that in mind, I turn in the final chapter from literature to music, with the recognition noted in advance that the portended liberation from the "text" is only provisional: that, after all, is what "the cunning of History" means.

CHAPTER 7

The Ideology of Postmodern Music and Left Politics

for Fred Jameson, in struggle

A dorno directed some of his most acid remarks on the sociology of music to the category of the "fan." For example:

> What is common to the jazz enthusiast of all countries is the moment of compliance, in parodistic exaggeration. In this respect their play recalls the brutal seriousness of the masses of followers in totalitarian states, even though the difference between play and seriousness amounts to that between life and death. . . . While the leaders in the European dictatorships of both shades raged against the decadence of jazz, the youth of the other countries has long since allowed itself to be electrified, as with marches, by the syncopated dance-steps, with bands which do not by accident stem from military music.[1]

One of the most important contributions of postmodernism has been, by contrast, its defense of an aesthetics of the *consumer.* The first thing to say, then, is that I am writing here as a "fan," a person who buys records or CDs and goes to concerts, not like Adorno from the perspective of the trained musician, composer, or musician-intellectual.

For Adorno, the development of modern music is a reflection of the decline of the bourgeoisie, whose most characteristic cultural medium, on the other hand, music is.[2] Christa Bürger recalls the essential image of the cultural in Adorno: that of Ulysses, who, tied to the mast of his ship, can listen to the song of the sirens while the slaves underneath work at the oars, cut off from the aesthetic experience that is reserved only for those in power.[3] What is implied and critiqued at the same time in the image is the stance of the traditional intellectual or aesthete in the face of the processes of transformation of culture into a commodity—mass culture—and the consequent collapse of the distinction between high and low culture, a collapse that defines the postmodern and that postmodernist ideology celebrates. In the postmodern mode, not only are Ulysses and his crew both listening to the siren song, they are singing along with it, as in "Sing Along with Mitch," and perhaps marking the beat with their oars: one-two, one-two, one-two-three-four.

* * *

One variant of the ideology of postmodern music may be illustrated by the following remarks from an interview John Cage gave in 1958 about his composition for electronic tape, *Fontana Mix*:

> *Q.*—I feel that there is a sense of logic and cohesion in your indeterminate music.
> *A.*—This logic was not put there by me, but was the result of chance operations. The thought that it is logical grows up in you . . . I think that all those things that we associate with logic and our observance of relationships, those aspects of our mind are extremely simple in relation to what actually happens, so that when we use our perception of logic we minimize the actual nature of the thing we are experiencing.
> *Q.*—Your conception (of indeterminacy) leads you into a universe nobody has attempted to charter before. Do you find yourself in it as a lawmaker?
> *A.*—I am certainly not at the point of making laws. I am more like a hunter, or an inventor, than a lawmaker.
> *Q.*—Are you satisfied with the way your music is made public—that is, by the music publishers, record companies, radio stations, etc.? Do you have complaints?
> *A.*—I consider my music, once it has left my desk, to be what in Buddhism would be called a non-sentient being . . . If someone kicked me—not my music, but me—then I might complain. But if they kicked my music, or cut it out, or don't play it enough, or too much, or something like that, than who am I to complain?[4]

By comparison, here is one of the great epiphanies of European literary modernism, the moment of the jazz song in Sartre's *Nausea*:

There is no melody, only notes, a myriad of tiny jolts. They know no rest, an inflexible order gives birth to them and destroys them without even giving them time to recuperate and exist for themselves. They race, they press forward, they strike me a sharp blow in passing and are obliterated. I would like to hold them back, but I know if I succeeded in stopping one it would remain between my fingers only as a raffish languishing sound. I must accept their death; I must even *will* it: I know few impressions stronger or more harsh.

I grow warm, I begin to feel happy. There is nothing extraordinary in this, it is a small happiness of Nausea: it spreads at the bottom of the viscous puddle, at the bottom of *our* time—the time of purple suspenders and broken chair seats; it is made of wide, soft instants, spreading at the edge, like an oil stain. No sooner than born, it is already old, it seems as though I have known it for twenty years. . . .

The last chord has died away. In the brief silence which follows I feel strongly that there it is, that *something has happened*.

Silence.

> *Some of these days*
> *You'll miss me honey*

What has just happened is that the Nausea has disappeared. When the voice was heard in the silence, I felt my body harden and the Nausea vanish. Suddenly: it was almost unbearable to become so hard, so brilliant. At the same time the music was drawn out, dilated, swelled like a waterspout. It filled the room with its metallic transparency, crushing our miserable time against the walls. I am *in* the music. Globes of fire turn in the mirrors; encircled by rings of smoke, veiling and unveiling the hard smile of light. My glass of beer has shrunk, it seems heaped up on the table, it looks dense and indispensable. I want to pick it up and feel the weight of it, I stretch out my hand . . . God! That is what has changed, my gestures. This movement of my arm has developed like a majestic theme, it has glided along the jazz song; I seem to be dancing.[5]

* * *

The passage from *Nausea* illustrates Adorno's dictum that music is the promise of redemption. This is what betrays its origins in those moments of ritual sacrifice and celebration in which the members of a human community are bonded or rebonded to their places within it. In *Nausea* the jazz song prefigures Roquentin's eventual reconciliation with his own self and his decision to write what is in effect his dissertation, a drama of choice that will not be unfamiliar to readers of this book. Even for an avant-gardist like Cage—in the allusion to Buddhism—music is still in some sense conceived as the sensuous form or "lived experience" of the religious.[6]

Was it not the function of music in relation to the great feudal ideologies—Islam, Christianity, Buddhism, Hinduism, Shintoism, Confucianism, and so on—to produce the sensation of the sublime and the eternal so as to constitute the image of the reward that awaited the faithful and obedient: the reward for submitting to exploitation or the reward for accepting the burden of exploiting? I am remembering as I write this Monteverdi's beautiful echo duet *Due Seraphim*—two angels—for the *Vespers of the Virgin Mary* of 1610, whose especially intense sweetness is perhaps related to the fact that it was written in a moment of crisis of both feudalism and Catholicism.

The Italian Mannerists in the early sixteenth century proclaimed the formal autonomy of the artwork from religious dogma. But if the increasing secularization of music in the European late Baroque and eighteenth century led on the one hand to the Jacobin utopianism of the *Ninth Symphony*, it produced on the other Kant's aesthetics of the sublime, that is, a mysticism of the bourgeois ego. Adorno understood that in modern music we are still in a domain where aesthetic experience, repression and sublimation, and class privilege and self-legitimation converge.[7]

* * *

Eugene Genovese pointed out in the Afro-American slave spiritual a different articulation of the relation of music and the religious than the one I have been suggesting: the sense in which both the music and the words of the song keep alive culturally the image of an imminent redemption from slavery and oppression, a redemption that lies within human time and a "real" geography of slave and free states ("The river Jordan is muddy and wide / Gotta get across to the other side").[8] Of the so-called Free Jazz movement of the sixties—Cecil Taylor, Ornette Coleman, Albert Ayler, John Coltrane, Archie Shepp, Sun Ra, and so on—the French critic Pierre Lere remarked (in a passage translated by Herbert Marcuse in one of his most influential essays on aesthetics and politics) that

> the liberty of the musical form is only the aesthetic translation of the will to social liberation. Transcending the tonal framework of the theme, the musician finds himself in a position of freedom. . . . The melodic line becomes the medium of communication between an initial order which is rejected and a final order which is hoped for. The frustrating possession of the one, joined with the liberating atttainment of the other, establishes a rupture in between the Weft of harmony which gives way to an aesthetic of the cry (*esthétique du cri*). This cry, the characteristic resonant (*sonore*) element of "free music," born in an exasperated tension, announces the violent rupture with the established white order and translates the advancing (*promotrice*) violence of a new black order.[9]

* * *

An ideology *of* music, then, but music itself as ideology, as an ideological practice? What I have in mind is not the problem, common to both a Saussurian and a vulgar Marxist musicology, of "how music expresses ideas." Jacques Attali has correctly observed that while music can be defined as noise given form according to a code, nevertheless it cannot be equated with a language. Music, though it has a precise operationality, never has stable reference to a semantic code of the linguistic type. It is a sort of language without meaning.[10]

Should we think of music, then, as outside of ideology (or the "outside" of ideology—I am referring to Althusser's dictum that ideology has no outside)? Galvano Della Volpe, in his *Critique of Taste*, pointedly excluded music (except for lyrics or words set to music) from the domain of ideology on the grounds of its nonverbal character; given their roots in linguistics and philosophy, poststructuralism in general and deconstruction in particular have also tended to see ideology as essentially bound up with language—the "Symbolic"—rather than organized states of feeling in general.[11] But we inhabit a cultural tradition also where it is something like a common-sense proposition that people listen to music precisely to escape from ideology, from the terrors of ideology and the dimension of practical reason. Thus Adorno, in what I take to be a quintessential modernist dictum, writes in *Aesthetic Theory*: "Beauty is like an exodus from the world of means and ends, the same world to which beauty owes its objective existence" (402).

Adorno and the Frankfurt School make of the Kantian notion of the aesthetic as the "disinterested" perception of a purposefulness without purpose precisely the locus of the radicalizing and redemptive power of art, the sense in which by alienating practical aims it sides with the repressed and challenges domination and exploitation, particularly the rationality of capitalist institutions. By contrast, there is Lenin's famous remark—it is in Gorky's *Reminiscences*—that he had to give up listening to Beethoven's *Appassionata* sonata: he enjoyed it too much; it made him feel soft, happy, at one with all humanity. Lenin's point would seem to be the need to resist a narcotic and pacifying aesthetic gratification in the name of the very difficult struggle—and the corresponding ideological and intellectual rigor—necessary to at least set in motion the process of building a society free of exploitation. But one senses in Lenin too the displacement or sublation of an aesthetic sensibility onto the field of revolutionary activism. And in both Adorno and Lenin there is a sense that music is in excess of ideology, its supplement.

Not only the Frankfurt School but most major tendencies in "Western Marxism" (the signal exception is Gramsci) maintain some form or other of the art/ideology distinction, with a characteristic ethical-epistemological privileging of the aesthetic *over* the ideological. In Althusser's early essays—"A Letter on Art to André Daspré," for example—art was said to occupy an intermediate position between science and ideology, since it involved ideology (as, so to speak, its raw material), but in such a way as to provoke an "internal distancing" from ideology, somewhat as in Brecht's notion of an "alienation effect" that obliges the spectator to scrutinize and question the assumptions on which the spectacle has been proceeding. In the section on interpellation in Althusser's later essay on ideology and ideological state apparatuses, this "modernist" concern with estrangement and dereification has been displaced by what is in effect a postmodernist concern with fascination and fixation. If ideology, in Althusser's central thesis in that essay, is what constitutes the subject in relation to the real, then its domain is not a worldview or set of (verbal) ideas, but rather the ensemble of signifying practices in societies: that is, culture as such.

* * *

If the aesthetic effect consists in a certain satisfaction of desire—a "pleasure" (in the formalists, the recuperation or production of sensation achieved by *ostranenie* or defamiliarization)—and if the aesthetic effect is an ideological effect, then the question becomes not the distinction between music and ideology but rather their relation. Music would seem, in this sense, to have a special relation to the preverbal, and thus to the Imaginary or, more exactly, to that special sense Kristeva gives to the term "the semiotic."[12] We take it (with apologies for the potted Lacanianism of cultural studies here) that objects of imaginary identification function in the psyche—in a manner Lacan himself designated as "orthopedic"—as metonyms of an object of desire that has been repressed or forgotten, a desire that can never be satisfied and that consequently inscribes in the subject a sense of insufficiency or fading. In narcissism, this desire takes the form of a libidinal identification of the ego with an image or sensation of itself as—according to Freud's tripartate demarcation of the alternatives in his 1916 essay on narcissism—it is, was, or should be. From the third of these possibilities—images or experiences of the ego as it should be—Freud argued that there arise as a consequence of the displacement of primary narcissism images of an ideal ego or ego ideal. Such images, however, are not only of self, but involve also the "social" ideals of the parent, the family, the tribe, the nation, the race, and so on (more accurately, they bind images of self to such ideals). Consequently, those sentiments that are the very stuff of ideology in the narrow sense of "isms" and loyalties—belonging to a party, being an American, defending the family honor, fighting in a national liberation movement—are basically transformations of homoerotic libidinal narcissism.

It follows that the aesthetic effect—even the sort of nonsemantic or iconic effect produced by the organization of sound in music—always implies a kind of social imaginary, a way of being with and/or for others. Although they are literature-centered, we may recall in this context Fredric

Jameson's remarks at the end of *The Political Unconscious* (in the section titled "The Dialectic of Utopia and Ideology") to the effect that "all class consciousness—that is, all ideology in the strict sense—as much the exclusive forms of consciousness of the ruling classes as the opposing ones of the oppressed classes, are in their very nature utopian." It follows for Jameson—this is his appropriation of Frankfurt aesthetics—that the aesthetic value of a given work of art can never be limited to its moment of genesis, when it functioned willy-nilly to legitimize some form or other of domination. For if its utopian quality as art—its "eternal charm," to recall Marx's (Eurocentric and petty bourgeois) remark on Greek epic poetry—is precisely that it expresses pleasurably the imaginary unity of a social collectivity, then "it is utopian not as a thing in itself, but rather to the extent that such collectivities are themselves ciphers for the final concretion of collective life, that is, the achieved utopia of a classless society."[13]

What this implies is that the political unconscious of the aesthetic is (the imaginary experience of) communism.

* * *

I want to introduce at this point an issue that was particularly crucial to the way in which I experienced and think about music, which is the relation between music and drugs. It is said that the passage from *Nausea* cited earlier derived from Sartre's experiments in the thirties with mescaline. Many readers will have their own versions of essential psychedelic experiences of the sixties; here is one of mine.

It is 1963, late at night. I'm a senior in college and I've taken peyote for the first time. I'm lying face down on a couch with a red velour cover in a friend's room. His pet ocelot is roaming around the floor. Mozart is playing, the slow movement of a piano concerto. As my nausea fades— peyote induces a very intense nausea in the first half hour or so—I begin to notice the music, which becomes increasingly clear and beautiful. I feel my breath making my body move against the couch and I feel the couch respond to me as if it were alive, very softly and gently. I remember or seem to remember being close to my mother's body in early childhood. I am overwhelmed with nostalgia. The room is flooded with light. I enter a timeless, paradisiacal state, beyond good and evil. The music goes on and on.

The downside of drugs was the freak-out or bad trip: the drug-exacerbated sensation that the music is incredibly banal and stupid, that the needle of the record player is covered with fuzz, that the sound is thick and ugly like mucus; Charles Manson hearing secret apocalyptic messages in "Helter Skelter" on the Beatles' *White Album*; the Rolling Stones at Altamont. Modernism in music, say, the infinitely compressed fragments of late Webern, is the perception—in the midst of the bad trip, of dissonance—of a momentary cohesion and radiance, whose power is all the greater because it shines out of chaos and evil. In Frankfurt aesthetics, dissonance is the voice of the oppressed in music. For Adorno it is only in dissonance, which destroys the illusion of reconciliation represented by harmony, that the power of seduction of the inspiring character of music survives (*Aesthetic Theory*, 21–22).

* * *

John Cage's *4'33"*—a piece where the performer sits at a piano without playing anything for four minutes and thirty-three seconds—is a sort of postmodernist homage to modernist aesthetics, to serialism and private-language musics. What it implies is that the listening subject is to compose the music from the very absence of music, the performance from the frustration of the expected performance. As in Duchamp's ready-mades or Rauschenberg's white paintings, Cage's induced silence gives rise to an appropriately "modernist" anxiety (which might be allegorized in Klee's twittering birds, whose noise emanates from the very miniaturization, compression, and silent tension of the pictorial space) to create an aesthetic experience out of the given, whatever it is.

Postmodernism per se in music, on the other hand, is where the anxiety of the listener to "make sense of" the piece is either perpetually frustrated by pure randomness— Cage's music of chance—or assuaged and dissipated by a minimalist, "easy-listening" surface with changes happening only in a Californian *longue durée*, as in the musics of La Monte Young, Philip Glass, Terry Riley, or Steve Reich. The intention of such musics, we might say, is to transgress both the Imaginary and the Symbolic: they are a sort of brainwashing into the Real.[14]

* * *

One form of capitalist utopia that is portended in contemporary music—we could call it the neoliberal or Chicago School version—is the record/CD store, with its incredible proliferation and variety of musical commodities, its promise of "different strokes for different folks," as Sly Stone would have it: Michael Jackson—or Prince, or Hammer— Liberace, Bach on original instruments or by the Philadelphia Orchestra, Heavy Metal—or Bruce Springsteen—country (what kind of country: Zydeco, Appalachian, bluegrass, Dolly Parton, trucker?), jazz, blues, spirituals, soul, rap, fusion, college rock (Grateful Dead, REM, Talking Heads), Seattle "grunge" rock, Holly Near, *Hymnen*, *salsa*, reggae, World Beat, *norteño* music, *cumbias*, Laurie Anderson, forty-six different recorded versions of *Bolero*, and so on, with the inevitable "crossovers" and "new waves." How could a "planned" production/distribution of music under socialism compete with this? (It is a sign of the speed of transformation in the music business that this list will be long out of date by the time this book is published.)

But this is surely also "Brazil" (the country and the song/ film): the dystopia of behaviorally tailored, industrially manufactured, packaged, and standardized music—Muzak— where it is expected that everyone except owners and managers of capital will be at the same time a low-wage fast-food-chain worker and consumer. Muzak is to music what McDonald's is to food; and since its purpose is to generate an environment conducive to both commodity production and consumption, it is more often than not to be heard in places like McDonald's (or, as we can read in prison testimonies, in that Latin American concomitant of neoliberalism which is the torture chamber, with the volume turned up to the point of distortion).

In Russell Berman's perhaps overly anxious image, Muzak implies a fundamental mutation of the public sphere, "the beautiful illusion of a collective, singing along in dictatorial unanimity." Its ubiquity, as in the parallel cases of advertising and packaging and design, refers to a situation where there is no longer "an outside to art. . . . There is no pre-aesthetic dimension to social activity, since the social order itself has become dependent on aesthetic organization."[15]

Berman's concern here is in the spirit of the critique that Habermas—and, in this country, Christopher Lasch—has made of postmodernism, a critique that coincides paradoxically with the cultural politics of the New Right (as evidenced, for example, in Allan Bloom's hysterical remarks on rock in *The Closing of the American Mind*). Is, however, the loss of autonomy of the aesthetic that Berman detects in contemporary consumer society a bad thing—something akin to Marcuse's notion of a "repressive desublimation" that entails the loss of art's critical potential? Could it not be seen instead as indicating a new vulnerability of capitalist societies—a need to relegitimize themselves through a general aestheticization of the life world—and therefore both a new *possibility* for the left and a new centrality for cultural and aesthetic matters in left practice?

As Berman notes, the aestheticization of everyday life was also the goal of the historical avant-garde in its attack on the institution of the autonomy of the aesthetic in bourgeois culture. The loss of aura or desublimation of the artwork may be a form of commodification, but it is also, as Walter Benjamin pointed out, a form of democratization of culture.[16] Cage writes suggestively in *Silence*, for example, of "a music which is like furniture—a music, that is, which will be part of the noises of the environment, will take them into consideration. I think of it as a melodious softening the noises of the knives and forks, not dominating them, not imposing itself. It would fill up those heavy silences that sometimes fall between friends dining together."[17] In the work of La Monte Young and Brian Eno, music becomes consciously an aspect of interior decorating. What this takes us back to, however, is not Muzak but the admirable Baroque tradition of *Tafelmusik*: "table" or dinner music. Mozart still wrote at the time of the French Revolution divertimenti meant to accompany social gatherings, including meetings of his Masonic lodge. After him, this utilitarian or "background" function is repressed in bourgeois art music, which will now require the deepest concentration and emotional and intellectual involvement on the part of the listening subject.

The problem with Muzak is not its ubiquity or the idea of environmental music per se, but rather its insistently kitsch melodic-harmonic content as orchestrated pop or "light" jazz. What is clear, on the other hand, is that that form of intense and informed concentration on the artwork that is assumed by Adorno and Frankfurt aesthetics depends on a privatized, bourgeois-Romantic, formalist conception of both music and the listening subject that is not unrelated to the actual processes of commodification that so-called classical music was undergoing in the late-eighteenth and nineteenth centuries (and to its role in the formation of modern bourgeois "national" culture).

*   *   *

The antidote to Muzak would seem to be something like Punk. By way of a preface to a discussion of Punk and extending the considerations above on the relation between music and commodification, I want to refer first to Jackson Pollock's painting *Autumn Rhythmn* in the Metropolitan Museum of Art in New York, a picture that—like Pollock's work in general—was particularly admired by Free Jazz musicians (a Pollock was featured on the cover of Ornette Coleman's canonic *Free Jazz* album). It is a vast painting with splotches of black, brown, and rust against the raw tan of unprimed canvas, with an incredible dancing, swirling, clustering, dispersing energy. As you look at it, you become aware that while the ambition of the painting seems to be to explode or expand the pictorial space of the canvas altogether, it is finally only the limits of the canvas that make the painting possible as an art object. The limit of the canvas is its aesthetic autonomy, its separation from the life world, but also its commodity status as something that can be bought, traded, exhibited. The commodity is implicated in the very form of the "piece"; as with the jazz record in *Nausea*, "The music ends." (The 78 RPM record—the commodity form of recorded early jazz in the twenties and thirties—imposed a three-minute limit per side on performances and this in turn shaped the way songs were arranged in jazz and pop recording; in rock, the same goes for the 45 and the idea of the "single," which persists in the format of MTV and music video shows on television.)

This sense of the bounded character of the artwork might indicate one limit of Jameson's cultural hermeneutic. If the strategy in Jameson is to uncover the emancipatory utopian-communist potential locked up in the artifacts of the cultural heritage, this is also in a sense to leave everything as it is, as in Wittgenstein's analytic (because that which is desired is already there; it only has to be "seen" correctly), whereas the problem of the relation of art and social liberation is also clearly the need to *transgress* the limits imposed by existing artistic forms and practices and to produce new ones. To the extent, however, such transgressions can be recontained within the sphere of the aesthetic—in a new series of "works" that may also be available as commodities—they will produce paradoxically an affirmation of bourgeois culture; in a certain sense they *are* bourgeois high culture.

A representation of this paradox in terms of sixties leftism is the great scene in Antonioni's *Zabriskie Point* where the young woman, indulging in a terrorist fantasy, imagines the desert home of the capitalist pig being blown up, and we see—in ultraslow motion, in Technicolor, accompanied by a spacey and sinister Pink Floyd music track—the whole commodity universe of late capitalism (cars, tools, supermarket food, radios, TVs, clothes, furniture, records, books, decorations, utensils) float by. What is not clear is who might have placed the bomb, however, so that Jameson might ask in reply a question the film itself also leaves unanswered: Is this an image of the destruction of capitalism or of its fission into a new and "higher" stage where it fills all space and time, where there is no longer something— nature, the Third World, the unconscious—outside it? And this question suggests another: To what extent was the cultural radicalism of the sixties, nominally directed against the rationality of capitalist society and its legitimating discourses, itself a form of modernization of capitalism, a prerequisite of its "expanded" reproduction in the new international division of labor and the proliferation of electronic technologies—with corresponding mind-sets—that emerged in the seventies and consolidated themselves in the age of Reagan?[18]

* * *

From Punk manifestos:[19]

Real life stinks.

What has been shown is that you and I can do anything in any area without training and with little cash.

We're demanding that real life keep up with advertising, the speed of advertising on TV . . . We are living at the speed of advertising. We demand to be entertained all the time, we get bored very quickly. When we're on stage, things happen a thousand times faster, everything we do is totally compressed and intense on stage, and that's our version of life as we feel and see it.

In the future T.V. will be so good that the printed word will function as an artform only. In the future we will not have time for leisure activities. In the future we will "work" one day a week. In the future there will be machines which will produce a religious experience in the user. In the future there will be so much going on that no one will be able to keep track of it. (David Byrne)

The emergence and brief hegemony of Punk—from, say, 1975 to 1982—was related to the very high levels of structural unemployment or subemployment that appeared in first world capitalist economies in the seventies as a consequence of the winding down of the post-World War II long cycle, and that imply, especially for lower-middle-class and working-class youth, a consequent displacement of the work ethic toward a kind of on-the-dole bohemianism or dandyism. Punk aimed at a sort of total spectacle or *Gesamtkunstwerk* (Simon Frith has noted its connections with Situationist ideology)[20] that would combine music, fashion, dance, speech forms, mime, graphics, criticism, new "on the street" forms of appropriation of urban space, and in which, in principle, everybody was both a performer and a spectator. Its key musical form was three-chord garage power rock, because its intention was to contest art rock and superstar rock, to break down the distance between fan and performer. Punk was loud, aggressive, eclectic, anarchic, amateur, self-consciously anticommercial and antihippie at the same time.

If the rise of Punk reflected the crisis of traditional white male working-class culture in the deep recessions and right-wing political realignment of the late seventies and early eighties, particularly in Great Britain, its limits were those defined by a still-expanding capitalist production of cultural commodities that it ultimately came to be part of. (In thinking the relation between postmodernism and post-fordism, it is tempting in fact to see this expansion of cultural production as an engineered compensation for the recessions that denied the working class the upward mobility it had previously won through trade-union struggles during the upward phase of the long cycle.) The most important of the Punk groups was the Sex Pistols, and it was the genius of their manager, the entrepreneur Malcolm McClaren, to know how to explore and exploit this paradoxical situation. Initially, Punk had to create its own forms of record production and distribution, independent of the "majors" and of commercial music institutions in general. But the moment—carefully prepared by McClaren's publicity work—when to be recognized as Punk was to conform to an established image of consumer desire was the moment Punk itself becomes a commodity. It is the moment depicted in the film *Sid and Nancy* of the Sex Pistols' U.S. tour, where, based on the realization that they are becoming a commercial success in the American market—*the* new band—they autodestruct. But the collapse of Punk—and its undoubted flirtation in some forms with nihilism and fascism—should not obscure the fact that it was for a while—most consciously in the work of groups like the Clash and in collective projects like Rock Against Racism—a very powerful form of left mass culture, perhaps—if we are attentive to the dictum that ideas acquire a material force when they reach the millions—one of the most powerful forms we have seen in recent years in Western Europe and the United States. The political force of Punk is matched today by the more radical rap groups like Public Enemy, and in certain forms of Heavy Metal (which, it should be recalled, has its roots in the Detroit sixties movement band, MC5).

* * *

The notion of postmodernism initially comes into play to designate a crisis in the dominant canons of American architecture. Hegel posited architecture over music as the world historical form of Romantic art, because in architecture the reconciliation of spirit and matter, reason and history, represented ultimately by the state, was more completely realized. Hence, Jameson's privileging of architecture in his various discussions of postmodernism. I think that today, however, particularly if we are concerned with developing a new form and practice of the left on the terrain of the postmodern, we have to be for music as against architecture, because it is in architecture that the power and self-representation of capital and the imperialist state reside, whereas music is always and everywhere a power of cultural production that is in the hands of the people. Capital can master and exploit music—and modern musics like rock are certainly forms of capitalist culture—but it can never seize hold of and monopolize its means of production (as the Spanish Baroque did with literature, for example).

The cultural presence of the Third World in and against the dominant of imperialism is, among other things, to borrow Attali's concept, "noise": the intrusion of new forms of language and music that imply new forms of community and pleasure. The debate some years ago over Paul Simon's album *Graceland* (which used South African township jive and choral music as a background for his own songs) shows that the simple presence of third world music in a first world context implies immediately a series of ideological effects, which does not mean that I think there is a "correct line" on *Graceland* (for example, that it is a case of third world misery and exploited labor sublimated into an item of first world white middle-class consumption). Whatever the problems with the concept of the Third World, it can no longer mark an "other" that is radically outside of and different from contemporary North American or European society. For a number of reasons, music has been and remains the dominant cultural form of this insertion.

* * *

Simon Frith has summarized succinctly the critique of the limitations of Frankfurt School aesthetic theory that I have been tracing:

> The Frankfurt scholars argued that the transformation of art into commodity inevitably sapped imagination and withered hope—now all that could be imagined was what was. But the artistic impulse is not destroyed by capital; it is transformed by it. As utopianism is mediated through the new processes of cultural production and consumption, new sorts of struggles over community and leisure begin.[21]

More and more—the point has been made by Claus Offe, among others—the survival of capitalism has become contingent on noncapitalist forms of culture, including those of the Third World. What is really utopian in the present context is not so much the sublation of art into life under the auspices of advanced consumer capitalism, but rather the neoliberal economic project of reabsorbing the entire life energy of global society into labor markets and industrial or service production. It is no wonder that the New Right cultural theorists seemed so deeply suspicious of and hostile to the very postmodernist art and fashion that, in Jameson's striking phrase, is the "cultural form" of the present stage of the capitalism they defend.[22] Nobody much wants to be considered a Marxist of any kind these days, but something very much akin to the famous contradiction between forces and relations of production is acutely evident in the current tensions—the FBI warning at the start of your evening video, for example—around the commercialization of VCR and digital sound technologies. Cheap computers, video recorders, and digital recorders are the latest hot electronic commodities, but they also portend the possibility of a virtual decommodification of music and film material, since its reproduction via these technologies can no longer be easily contained within the "normal" boundaries of capitalist property relations (which, Marx reminded us, are ultimately bound up with the relations of production themselves).

As opposed to both Frankfurt School-style angst about commodification and a left neopopulism that cannot imagine anything finer than Bruce Springsteen (I have in mind something like Jesse Lemisch's polemic against Popular Front-style "folk" music in the *Nation* some years ago),[23] we should reject the notion that certain kinds of music are per se ethically and politically correct and others not. Old Left versions of this ranged from jazz = good ("people's music"), classical = bad (American CP), to jazz = bad ("decadent"), classical = good (Soviet CP). (This is not to say that particular songs or compositions should not be subjected to ideological analysis and critique.) The position of the left today—understanding the left in the broadest possible sense, as in the idea of the Rainbow—should be in favor of the broadest possible variety and proliferation of musics and related technologies of pleasure, on the understanding, or hope, that in the long run this will be deconstructive of capitalist hegemony.

This is a postmodernist position, but it also involves challenging a certain smugness in postmodernist theory and practice about just how far elite/popular, high culture/mass culture distinctions have broken down. Too much of what gets called postmodernism is simply a renovated form of bourgeois avant-garde "art" culture: that is, modernism under another brand name. Russell Berman worries about the loss of art's negative potential with cultural commodification. But the real problem is not how much, but rather how little, this commodification has introduced an aestheticization of everyday life. The left, on the other hand, which—particularly in certain of its reformist modes—seems to be competing with neoliberalism for the job of renovating capitalism, needs to identify itself with the pleasure principle ("fun") represented, partially and in alienated forms, by late-capitalist commodity culture, and develop around this identification effective images and experiences of *postcommodity* gratification, linked as transitional demands to a general expansion of leisure time and a consequent transformation of the welfare state from the realm of economic maintenance (the famous "safety net") to that of pleasure and personal development outside the parameters of commodity production. While it is good and necessary to remind ourselves that we have come a long way from the cultural forms championed by the Popular Fronts of the thirties—that these are now the stuff of *our mode rétro*—we also

need to think about the ways that they were able to hege-
monize both mass and elite culture in their day (Woody
Guthrie was not only a "folk" artist; he had a popular
country-music radio show that covered Los Angeles and the
Southwest). The creation—as, in a tentative way, in this
chapter—of an *ideologeme* that articulates the political project
of ending or attenuating capitalist domination with both the
production *and* consumption of contemporary music seems
to me one of the most important tasks in cultural work that
the left should have on its agenda.

Of course, what we anticipate in taking up this task is also
the moment—or moments—when architecture becomes the
form of expression of the people, because that would be the
moment when power had really begun to change hands.
What would this architecture consist in?

Notes

Preface

1. Gayatri Spivak, "Interview with *Radical Philosophy*," *The Post-Colonial Critic* (New York and London: Routledge, 1990), p. 134.
2. John Beverley and Marc Zimmerman, *Literature and Politics in the Central American Revolutions* (Austin: University of Texas Press, 1990), p. 207.
3. Mary Louise Pratt, "Arts of the Contact Zone," *Profession 91* (1991), pp. 33–40.

Chapter 1. "By Lacan": From Literature to Cultural Studies

1. Gayatri Spivak, "Reading the World," in *In Other Worlds: Essays in Cultural Politics* (New York and London: Methuen, 1987), p. 95.
2. "It is, however, the great and exemplary value of both Lacan and Derrida that in their quarrel with each other they do more than scrupulously restrict their readings of the central topoi of western self-reflexive language to the level of generality appropriate to the register of allegorical abstraction called for by such massive metaphoremes and motifs. In addition, they recognize this level of generality for what it is: the logic of the literary word in the west. Doing so, they open up the possibility of an extraliterary reading of literature." Joel Fineman, *The Subjectivity Effect in Western Literary Tradition: Essays Toward the Release of Shakespeare's Will* (Cambridge, Mass.: MIT Press, 1991), pp. 140–41.
3. Tony Bennett, "Texts in History: The Determination of Readings and Their Texts," *Journal of the Midwest Modern Language Association* 18, 1 (1985), p. 10. The concept is intended as an alternative to phenomenologically oriented reception or reader-response theory of the sort represented by Gadamer or Stanley Fish.
4. Angel Rama, *La ciudad letrada* (Hanover, N.H.: Ediciones del Norte, 1984).
5. This has been the subject of much recent work in Latin American criticism, of which I might single out Alejandro Losada's essays, collected posthumously in *La literatura en la sociedad de América Latina* (Aarhus, Denmark: Romansk Institut Aarhus Universitet, 1981); Benedict Anderson, *Imagined Communities: Reflections on the Origin and Spread of Nationalism* (London: Verso, 1983); Roberto González Echevarría, *The*

143

Voice of the Masters: Writing and Authority in Modern Latin American Literature (Austin: University of Texas Press, 1985); Jean Franco, *Plotting Women: Gender and Representation in Mexican Literature* (New York: Columbia University Press, 1989); Doris Sommer, *Foundational Fictions* (Berkeley: University of California Press, 1991); and Julio Ramos, *Desencuentros de la modernidad en América Latina: Literatura y política en el siglo XIX* (Mexico City: Fondo de Cultura Económica, 1989), which I discuss in detail below.

6. The exception, paradoxically, given his conservative politics, was Borges: see, for example, his story "El Sur," which is a highly literary version of the disintegration of the "ciudad letrada." A good overview of the Boom and the literary and political ideologies that animated it is Gerald Martin, *Journeys through the Labyrinth* (London: Verso, 1989).

7. Roberto Fernández Retamar, *Caliban and Other Essays*, trans. Edward Baker (Minneapolis: University of Minnesota Press, 1989).

8. Nelson Osorio, *Revista de crítica literaria latinoamericana* 29 (1989), p. 215.

9. Jean Baudrillard, *In the Shadow of the Silent Majorities* (New York: Semiotext[e], 1983), pp. 43–44. On postmodernist "reception," the key essay is Jane Feuer, "Reading *Dynasty*: Television and Reception Theory," *South Atlantic Quarterly* 88, 2 (Spring 1989).

10. Julio Ramos, *Desencuentros de la modernidad en América Latina: Literatura y política en el siglo XIX*. The translations from the text that follow are mine. The reader should keep in mind that *modernismo* is not exactly commensurate as either a period- or style-concept with modernism in English. The nearer, but still not quite exact, Spanish equivalent for that is *vanguardismo* (Borges, for example, is a *vanguardista*, not a *modernista*).

11. This debate sometimes verged on the hysterical: thus the distinguished historian C. Vann Woodward delivered himself in the pages of the *New York Review* (July 18, 1991) of the opinion that after the death of her parents at the hands of the Guatemalan army Rigoberta Menchú "turned against European culture, renounced marriage and motherhood, and became a feminist and a Marxist." Called to task on each of these points in a letter in a subsequent issue of the journal by Professor Gene Bell-Villada of Williams College, Woodward admitted that he had not actually read *I, Rigoberta Menchú* but had depended on D'Souza's characterization of it in *Illiberal Education* (*NYR*, September 26, 1991, pp. 74–76). So much for the vaunted empiricism of the American historical profession! D'Souza noted apropos the awarding of the Nobel Peace Prize to Menchú: "I was slightly consternated that she won . . . , though I was relieved that she didn't win for literature" (*Chronicle of Higher Education*, October 28, 1992, p. A6).

12. Richard Rodriguez, *Hunger of Memory: The Education of Richard Rodriguez* (New York: Bantam Books, 1983).

13. Gayatri Spivak, interviewed by Howard Winant, "On the Politics of the Subaltern," *Socialist Review* 90, 3 (1990), p. 91.
14. Walter Benjamin, *The Origin of German Tragic Drama*, trans. John Osborne (London: New Left Books, 1977), p. 106.
15. Michael Nerlich, "Toward a Nonliterary Understanding of Literature: Reflections on the Notion of the 'Popular,' " in *Literature among the Discourses: The Spanish Golden Age*, ed. Wlad Godzich and Nicholas Spadaccini (Minneapolis: University of Minnesota Press, 1986), p. 78.
16. "Both varidisciplinarity and interdisciplinarity models (like political pluralism) are modes of eclecticism—forms of (ack)knowledgement accumulating knowledge without having to confront the ideology of the production of knowledge. Transdisciplinarity, on the other hand, is aware of the status of knowledge as of the modes of the ideological construction of reality in any given discipline and thus through its self-reflexivity attempts not simply to accumulate knowledge but to ask what constitutes knowledge, why and how and by whose authority certain modes of understanding are certified as knowledge. . . . Transdisciplinarity is a '*transgressive*' space in which configurations of knowledges are displayed as ultimately power-related." Mas'ud Zavarzadeh and Donald Morton, "Theory Pedagogy Politics: The Crisis of 'The Subject' in the Humanities," *boundary 2* 15, 1–2 (1986/87). Zavarzadeh and Morton credit this distinction in turn to Teresa Ebert.
17. Stuart Hall puts his finger on what I think is the main problem entailed in the "interdisciplinary" institutionalization of cultural studies. Admitting that even as coherent a model of cultural studies as the practice of the Birmingham School was constructed out of radically different conjunctures, concerns, methodologies, and theoretical positions (which would seem to suggest that the organization of the field must be an "open-ended" one), he asks: "Does it follow that cultural studies is not a policed disciplinary area? That it is whatever people do, if they choose to call or locate themselves within the project and practice of cultural studies? I am not happy with that formulation either. Although cultural studies as a project is open-ended, it can't be simply pluralist in that way. Yes, it refuses to be a master discourse or a meta-discourse of any kind. Yes, it is a project that is always open to that which it doesn't yet know, to that which it can't yet name. But it does have some will to connect; it does have some stake in the choices it makes. It does matter whether cultural studies is this or that. It can't be just any old thing which chooses to march under a particular banner. It is a serious enterprise, or project, and that is inscribed in what is sometimes called the 'political' aspect of cultural studies." Stuart Hall, "Cultural Studies and its Theoretical Legacies," in *Cultural Studies*, ed. Lawrence Grossberg, Cary Nelson, and Paula Treichler (New York: Routledge, 1992), p. 278.
18. See, for example, Jonathan Arac, "Nationalism, Hypercanonization, and *Huckleberry Finn*," *boundary 2* 19, 1 (1992); Beatriz González Ste-

phan, *La historiografía literaria del liberalismo hispanoamericana del siglo XIX* (Havana: Casa de las Américas, 1987); Peter Hohendahl, *Building a National Literature: The Case of Germany, 1830–1870*, (Ithaca N.Y.: Cornell University Press, 1989); and Gregory Jusdanis, *Belated Modernity and Aesthetic Culture: Inventing National Literature* (Minneapolis: University of Minnesota Press 1991).

Chapter 2. The Formation of the Ideology of the Literary (from Garcilaso to Greenblatt)

1. "In a culture that is no longer sign-like or communal, messages become fragmented because the addressee is no longer homogenous. . . . The emergent state bureaucracy, having abandoned Latin, favors one sociolect, and, within it, one discourse (or style as it is known at the time), and makes all others answerable to it. Henceforth all dealings that involve interdiscursive crossing must be mediated by the dominant discourse. . . . The individual discourses lose their autonomy and, as a result of being integrated into the state's totalization, their self-sufficiency as well. They are now fragments of a much larger whole, patches of a great quilt. Their speakers lose their autonomy and self-sufficiency, and must recognize that they are speakers of fragmentary discourses which can never be totalized. Only the state can achieve this totalization—at least such is the claim. There is a striking similarity between this claim and what the novel does. *Don Quijote* is paradigmatic in this respect. Its famous dialogical structure represents an attempt to inscribe as many discourses as possible within its frame. *The question is who can read them. In a sense, the answer is: the state.* Only the totalizing state can claim to be the adequate subject for reading a novel like the *Quijote*. . . . In practice this means that such a novel serves to provide its readers with an experience of what it is to look at things from the perspective of the state, that is, to perceive the limitations of each of the individual discourses and the configuration of their addition. At the same time, it demonstrates powerfully the inordinateness of the state's claim and the impossibility of its realization." Wlad Godzich and Nicholas Spadaccini, "Popular Culture and Spanish Literary History," in the volume also edited by them, *Literature among the Discourses: The Spanish Golden Age* (Minneapolis: University of Minnesota Press, 1986), pp. 54, 59–61; emphasis mine).
2. Gauri Viswanathan, *Masks of Conquest: Literary Study and British Rule in India* (New York: Columbia University Press, 1991), p. 3.
3. The key study in this respect is Partha Chatterjee, *Nationalist Thought in the Colonial World—A Derivative Discourse* (London: Zed, 1986).
4. Roland Greene, "For Love of *Pau-Brasil*: Petrachan Experience and the Colonial Americas," paper presented at The English Institute, 1990. Cited from author's manuscript.
5. Richard Kagan, "Las universidades en Castilla, 1500–1700," in *Poder y*

sociedad en la España de los Austrias, ed. John H. Elliott (Barcelona: Editorial Crítica, 1982).

6. Paul Otto Kristeller, *The Classics and Renaissance Thought* (Cambridge, Mass.: Harvard University Press, 1955).

7. Anthony Grafton and Lisa Jardine, *From Humanism to the Humanities: Education and the Liberal Arts in Fifteenth- and Sixteenth-Century Europe* (London: Duckworth, 1986), pp. xiii–xiv.

8. Stephen Greenblatt, whose own work I will turn to shortly, has captured better the sense of what I want to say here in his remarks on Joel Fineman's studies of Shakespeare's sonnets: "For it is in Shakespeare's sonnets, Fineman sought to demonstrate, that the literary formation of the self in the slippage from presence to representation finds definitive expression, and it is in the sonnets too that the desire of the homosexual for the heterosexual finds its most powerful and poignant voice. . . . Homosexual desire in the young man sonnets is visual and visionary desire, based on an idealized homology between signifier and signified, the exhibition of praise and the perfect object of that praise. Heterosexual desire in the dark lady sonnets is, by contrast, self-consciously and explicitly verbal; it represents a fall into language that conceals as much as it shows, that has as its object a beloved characterized by her inadequacy and deceptiveness. This desire, writes Fineman, is a 'desire *of* language,' that is, both a craving for words and a craving generated by words." Stephen Greenblatt, "Introduction: Joel Fineman's 'Will,' " in Joel Fineman, *The Subjectivity Effect in Western Literary Tradition* (Cambridge, Mass.: MIT Press, 1991), pp. xiii–xiv.

9. See, for example, Catherine Belsey, *The Subject of Tragedy: Identity and Difference in Renaissance Drama* (London and New York: Methuen, 1985).

10. See Hugh Honour, *The New Golden Land: European Images of America from the Discoveries to the Present Time* (New York: Pantheon, 1975), pp. 84–117.

11. Stephen Greenblatt, *Marvelous Possessions: The Wonder of the New World* (Chicago: University of Chicago Press, 1991).

12. Tzvetan Todorov, *The Conquest of America*, trans. Richard Howard (New York: Harper & Row, 1984).

13. Gayatri Spivak, "French Feminism in an International Frame," in *In Other Worlds* (New York: Methuen, 1987), pp. 136–41. In the Romantics, the sublime is the experience of a spectacle in nature that is awe-inspiring rather than merely pretty: Niagara Falls as opposed to the pastoral, for example. But, by a curious paradox Kant identified in his distinction of the sublime and the beautiful, whereas beauty refers to the properties of something outside ourselves ("the form of the *finality* of an object in so far as it is perceived in that object without its end being represented"), the sublime, though it may be elicited by an object of perception outside the self, is actually an experience of self that transcends the object. "Sublimity therefore does not reside in any of

the things of nature, but only in our own mind, in so far as we may
become conscious of our superiority over nature within, and thus also
over nature without." Immanuel Kant, *The Critique of Judgement*, trans.
James Meredith (Oxford: Clarendon Press, 1952), p. 114.

14. Donald Pease, in *Consequences of Theory*, ed. Jonathan Arac and Barbara Johnson (Baltimore: Johns Hopkins University Press, 1989),
p. 138.

15. Fredric Jameson, *Postmodernism; or, The Cultural Logic of Late Capitalism*
(Durham, N.C.: Duke University Press, 1991), p. 189.

16. Although I do not want to assimilate their projects to Greenblatt's
(about which they have expressed their own reservations), I find a
trace of this same aesthetics of the sublime in the work of Rolena
Adorno and Beatriz Pastor on the representation of New World alterity. Both have written on Álvar Núñez Cabeza de Vaca's *Naufragios*, a
text that has become something of a touchstone for work on Spanish
colonial literature in a feminist or poststructuralist vein: Adorno in
"The Negotiation of Fear in Cabeza de Vaca's *Naufragios*," in the journal of record of the new historicism, *Representations* 33 (Winter 1991),
pp. 163-99; Pastor in her book *Discurso narrativo de la Conquista de
América* (Havana: Casa de las Américas, 1983). Adorno foregrounds
the figuration in the *Naufragios* of the immediacy and urgency of cultural negotiation implied by the desperate situation from which
Cabeza de Vaca narrates (which, she observes, disappears in the incorporation of the narrative into the official histories or *crónicas* of the
Conquest). Pastor reads the text as a "narrative of failure" (*narrativa
del fracaso*) that breaks down the hierarchical and teleological assumptions of epic narrative paradigms and opens up the possibility of a
more humanized experience of the other.

What Adorno also notes in her paper, however, is that what she
and Pastor see in the *Naufragios* as a deconstructive and radicalizing
experience of otherness—which in its textual form is fundamentally
an aesthetic one—is also an *alternative model of colonization*. This becomes clear in the later stages of the *Naufragios* (but it is precisely narrative teleology that the new historicism, as we have seen, is wont to
suspend), where the narrator tells how he was able to resettle and
organize Indian communities in northwestern Mexico that had been
driven off by the military depradations of a previous conquistador,
Nuño de Guzmán. This is not a model of decolonization, but rather
of a more sensitive and flexible form of colonial control, adapted not
so much to conquest as to the subsequent project of what Latin American historians call "colonial stabilization," and founded to a certain
extent on the very qualities the *Naufragios* as a literary text enacts. Like
Greenblatt with his "traveler's anecdotes" in *Marvelous Possessions*,
Adorno and Pastor are themselves within the ideology of the literary
that the *Naufragios* enacts as an effective practice of colonial hegemony. The resulting overvaluing of the aesthetic, the liminal, the nonteleological, the "cultural" produces a feminized, but not necessarily

a feminist, critique of colonial power. I would make much the same point about Homi Bhabha's influential essays on the cultural dynamics of postcoloniality, which seem, for all their theoretical sophistication and complexity, to involve a relatively straightforward recasting of modernist aestheticism as resistance and decolonization.

Chapter 3. On the Spanish Literary Baroque

1. Walter Benjamin, *The Origin of German Tragic Drama*, trans. John Osborne (London: New Left Books, 1977), p. 98.
2. Werner Weisbach, *Der Barock als Kunst der Gegenreformation* (Berlin: P. Cassirer, 1921).
3. This is an issue similar to the revival of Baroque instruments and performance practices in early modern music; that is, it involves attention to *ideologies* of textual determination and interpretation.
4. Nor, of course, was it the case that all "Spaniards" were even Spanish speakers in the sixteenth and seventeenth centuries: Spanish is a modernized form of Castilian, one of seven major languages used on the Iberian peninsula at the time (Arabic, Hebrew, Basque, Portuguese, Galician, and Catalan were the others).
5. "Popular Culture and Spanish Literary History," in *Literature among the Discourses: The Spanish Golden Age*, ed. Wlad Godzich and Nicholas Spadaccini (Minneapolis: University of Minnesota Press, 1986), p. 47. Apropos the "neobaroque" style of the Italian Modernist poet Ungaretti, Gramsci observed: "We might note, however, that the classical baroque, sadly, was and is popular (it is well-known that the man of the people likes the acrobatics of images in poetry), while the current baroque style is popular among pure intellectuals. Ungaretti has written that his comrades in the trenches, who were 'common people,' liked his poems, and it may be true: a particular kind of liking to do with the feeling that 'difficult' (incomprehensible) poetry must be good and its author a great man precisely because he is detached from the people and incomprehensible." Antonio Gramsci, *Selections from Cultural Writings*, ed. David Forgacs and Geoffrey Nowell-Smith (London: Lawrence and Wishart, 1985), pp. 272–73.
6. Noam Chomsky, *Cartesian Linguistics* (New York: Harper, 1966); see also chapters 2 and 3 of Michel Foucault's *Les Mots et les choses* (Paris: Gallimard, 1966). Like Cervantes, who used it to create the character of Tomás in *El licenciado Vidriera*, Gracián would have been intimately familiar with Huarte de San Juan's *Examen de ingenios* (c. 1580), a treatise on the nature of intelligence that, according to Chomsky, was one of the founding texts of the new school.
7. José Antonio Maravall, *Culture of the Baroque: Analysis of a Historical Structure*, trans. Terry Cochran (Minneapolis: University of Minnesota Press, 1986).
8. Parker explains that "by 'objects' [Gracián] understands not only material objects but also any object of thought: abstraction, attribute, re-

lation (including coincidence, contradiction), etc. The verbal formulation of the concept is the 'objective' (and subtle) expression of the
Wit. The latter is *artificiosa*, in the sense of not being the product of
the intellect's natural functioning but an 'artistic' act of the *ingenio*—
the intellect functioning imaginatively and aesthetically. An 'artificial'
(rather than natural or objective correspondence), says Gracián, is the
determining feature of any kind of Wit." A. A. Parker, *Polyphemus and
Galatea: A Study in the Interpretation of a Baroque Poem* (Austin: University of Texas Press, 1977), p. 21. That what is involved in Gracián's
definition of the *concepto* is a specifically aesthetic form of perception
(in something close to the later Kantian distinction of aesthetic and
teleological judgment) Gracián makes clear in another passage of the
Agudeza: "Wit does not content itself with truth alone, but also aspires
to beauty. It would be of little consequence to assure the stability in
the architecture if one did not also attend to the ornamentation" ("No
se contenta el ingenio con sola la verdad, como el juicio, sino aspira
a la hermosura. Poco fuera en la arquitectura asegurar firmeza, si no
atendiera al ornato").

9. David Hildner, "Aristocracy and Reason: Behavior Patterns in Calderón's Secular Characters," *Ideologies and Literature* 13 (1980), pp.
51-52.

10. Dámaso Alonso, *Góngora y el "Polifemo"* II (Madrid: Gredos, 1967), pp.
44-45: "Yo había interpretado que los 'lazos de oro' tenían dos fines:
el resaltar, en cuanto 'de oro', la blancura de la nieve de Angélica, y
el impedir, en cuanto 'lazos', que 'la hermosura del orbe', Angélica,
pudiera huirse (hay que recordar la índole huidiza y trotamundos que
en la obra de Ariosto tiene la asendereada muchacha)."

11. I depend here on Nikos Poulantzas's brilliant discussion of these matters in *State, Power, and Socialism* (London: New Left Books, 1978).

12. Clifford Geertz, *Negara: The Theatre State in Seventeenth-Century Bali*
(Princeton: Princeton University Press, 1980), p. 13.

13. John Merrington, "Town and Country in the Transition to Capitalism," in *The Transition from Feudalism to Capitalism*, ed. Rodney Hilton
(London: New Left Books, 1976), p. 171.

14. J. H. Elliott, "Concerto Barroco," *New York Review of Books* (April 9,
1987), pp. 26-29.

15. On this point see Miguel Batllori, "La barroquización de la *ratio
studiorum*" and "Gracián y la retórica barroca" in his *Gracián y el barroco* (Rome: Edizioni di Storia e Letteratura, 1958), and R. Wittkower,
Baroque Art: The Jesuit Contribution (New York: Fordham University
Press, 1972).

16. J. H. Elliott, "Self-Perception and Decline in Early Seventeenth Century Spain," *Past and Present* 74 (1977), p. 48.

17. On the theme of entropy in Baroque representation, Benjamin wrote:
"This is the heart of the allegorical way of seeing, of the baroque,
secular explanation of history as the Passion of the world; its importance lies solely in the stations of its decline. The greater the significance, the greater the subjection to death, because death digs most

deeply the jagged line of demarcation between physical nature and significance. But if nature has always been subject to the power of death, it is also true that it has always been allegorical. Significance and death both come to fruition in historical development, just as they are closely linked as seeds in the creature's graceless state of sin" (*Origin*, 106).

18. See Clastres's essay on ethnocide in *Recherches d'anthropologie politique* (Paris: Seuil, 1980).

19. In Forgacs and Nowell-Smith, eds., *Selections from Cultural Writings*, p. 234.

20. Glossing this point, David Forgacs remarks that "whereas in the other European countries the exported Renaissance produced a progressive scientific intelligentsia, which played a crucial role in the formation of the modern national states, in Italy itself it led to the involutionary Counter-Reformation and the ideological triumph of the Catholic intellectual hierarchy." David Forgacs, "National-Popular: Genealogy of a Concept," in *Formations of Nations and People*, ed. Tony Bennett (London: Routledge, 1984), p. 79.

21. It is this second face of Spanish Baroque culture, where the strategies it deploys to repress and recontain modernity produce unintended or unmastered effects, that is the focus of Walter Cohen's revision of the ideological consequences of the *comedia*, *The Drama of a Nation: Public Theater in Renaissance Spain and England* (Ithaca, N.Y.: Cornell University Press, 1985). Against the assumption by Maravall that Baroque public theater made a "consistent, self-conscious double appeal—one to the vulgar and unlettered, the other to the refined and erudite," Cohen counters that this "reduces the audience to ideological passivity and victimization, despite abundant contemporary evidence to the contrary and despite the only partial success of the far more effectively manipulative electronic media of the twentieth century in achieving this end." It also "falsifies the experience of the plays, many of which create complex effects that derive in significant part from popular culture" (169). Cohen is not unaware of the overwhelmingly conservative character of the overt message of the plays, but he also notes the possible slippage between intention and reception: "The public theaters constituted part of both the base and the superstructure, their function in one conflicting with their role in the other. . . . The medium and the message were in contradiction, a contradiction that resulted above all from the popular contribution" (183). For related perspectives, see, for example, Paul Julian Smith, "Barthes, Góngora, and Non-sense," *PMLA* 101, 1 (1986); the acts of a 1981 colloquium on *La Contestation de la Société dans la Littérature Espagnole du siècle D'or* (Toulouse: Université de Toulouse, 1981); or the collection in which this essay originally appeared, *Culture and Control in Counter-Reformation Spain*, ed. Anne J. Cruz and Mary Elizabeth Perry (Minneapolis: University of Minnesota Press, 1992).

22. Michel Foucault, *Power/Knowledge: Selected Interviews and Other Writings* (New York: Pantheon, 1980), p. 119.

Chapter 4. The Margin at the Center: On Testimonio

1. Raymond Williams, "The Writer: Commitment and Alignment," *Marxism Today* 24 (June 1980), p. 25.
2. See Miguel Barnet, "La novela-testimonio. Socioliteratura," which became a sort of manifesto for testimonio, originally published in the journal of the Cuban Writer's Union, *Unión*, and reprinted in *Testimonio y literatura*, ed. René Jara and Hernán Vidal (Minneapolis: Institute for the Study of Ideologies and Literature, 1986).
3. On guerrilla testimonio, see Juan Duchesne, "Las narraciones guerrilleras: configuración de un sujeto épico de nuevo tipo," in *Testimonio y literatura*, pp. 137–85); John Beverley and Marc Zimmerman, *Literature and Politics in the Central American Revolutions* (Austin: University of Texas Press, 1990), pp. 172–211; and Barbara Harlow, *Resistance Literature* (New York: Methuen, 1987).
4. One of the most important protagonists of testimonio has been the socialist-feminist poet Margaret Randall, who worked in Cuba and Nicaragua conducting workshops to train people to collect their own experience and begin building popular histories written or composed by themselves. She is the author of a very useful handbook on how to make a testimonio, *Testimonios: A Guide to Oral History* (Toronto: Participatory Research Group, 1985), and has edited a number of testimonios on the role of women in Latin American political struggle, including *Cuban Women Now* (Toronto: Women's Press, 1974) and *Sandino's Daughters* (Vancouver: New Star, 1983).
5. René Jara, "Prólogo," *Testimonio y literatura*, p. 3.
6. Hans Robert Jauss, "Ursprung und Bedeutung der Ichform im *Lazarillo de Tormes*," *Romanisches Jahrbuch* 10 (1959), pp. 297–300.
7. Rigoberta Menchú, with Elisabeth Burgos-Debray, *I, Rigoberta Menchú: An Indian Woman in Guatemala*, trans. Ann White (London: Verso, 1984), p. 1.
8. For example, the extraordinary multivoice and polyglot testimonio created by the Jamaican women's theater collective Sistren, with Honor Ford-Smith, *Lionheart Gal: Life Stories of Jamaican Women* (Toronto: Women's Press, 1986), which I'm grateful to Robert Carr for telling me about.
9. See Jameson's idea of a postbourgeois "*collective subject*, decentered but not schizophrenic. It emerges in certain forms of storytelling that can be found in third-world literature, in testimonial literature, in gossip and rumors and things of this kind. It is a storytelling which is neither personal in the modernist sense, nor depersonalized in the pathological sense of the schizophrenic text." Anders Stephanson, "Regarding Postmodernism: A Conversation with Fredric Jameson," *Social Text* 17 (1987), p. 45.
10. The most dramatic case of this insistence that I know of occurs in the Egyptian testimonial novel *Woman at Point Zero* (London: Zed, 1983), where the narrator is a young prostitute about to be executed for murdering her pimp. Her interlocutor—the Egyptian feminist writer Nawal El Saadawi—was at the time the prison psychiatrist. The pros-

titute, Firdaus, begins by addressing this person—who represents, albeit in a benevolent form, both the repressive power of the state and the institution of literature—as follows: "Let me speak! Do not interrupt me! I have no time to listen to you. They are coming to take me at six o'clock this evening. Tomorrow morning I shall no longer be here" (11). Barbara Harlow (*Resistance Literature*, pp. 139–40) notes that El Saadawi was herself imprisoned by the Sadat regime for feminist activities some years after this meeting and wrote an account of her experience, *Memoirs from the Women's Prison.*

11. Eliana Rivero, "Testimonios y conversaciones como discurso literario," in *Literature and Contemporary Revolutionary Culture*, ed. Hernán Vidal (Minneapolis: Society for the Study of Contemporary Hispanic and Lusophone Revolutionary Literatures, 1984–85), pp. 218–28 (translation mine). Cabezas tape-recorded himself telling stories of the guerrilla (usually with a friend in the room) and then edited the resulting transcript, acting as his own interlocutor.

12. In cases where testimonios are more directly part of political or social activism—for example, in the use of testimonio in liberation theology base community dialogues or as a kind of cadre literature—these editorial functions are often handled directly by the party or movement in question, constituting then not only a new literary form but also new, noncommodified forms of literary production and distribution.

13. K. Millet, "Framing the Narrative: The Dreams of Lucinda Nahuelhaul," in *Poética de la población marginal*, ed. James Romano (Minneapolis: Prisma Institute, 1987), pp. 425, 427.

14. For example: "Of course, I'd need a lot of time to tell you all about my people, because it's not easy to understand just like that. And I think I've given some idea of that in my account. Nevertheless, I'm still keeping my Indian identity a secret. I'm still keeping secret what I think no one should know. Not even anthropologists or intellectuals, no matter how many books they have, can find out all our secrets." *I, Rigoberta Menchú*, p. 247.

15. See Mao Tse-tung, "On the Correct Handling of Contradictions Among the People" (1957); see also Ernesto Laclau's influential discussion of the people/power bloc distinction in his essay "Towards a Theory of Populism," in *Politics and Ideology in Marxist Theory* (London: New Left Books, 1977).

16. Relevant here are the concerns expressed in the essays in James Clifford and George Marcus's *Writing Culture* (Berkeley: University of California Press, 1986), particularly Mary Louise Pratt's "Fieldwork in Common Places."

17. Elzbieta Sklodowska, "La forma testimonial y la novelística de Miguel Barnet," *Revista/Review Interamericana* 12, 3 (1982), p. 379 (my translation).

18. This may be as good a place as any to note the difference between my sense of testimonio and what Barbara Foley does in *Telling the Truth: The Theory and Practice of Documentary Fiction* (Ithaca, N.Y.: Cornell University Press, 1986). Some of the texts Foley discusses are in fact

testimonios, not novels, but the force of her argument is more to deconstruct what she calls the "fact/fiction distinction" as such. Thus, documentary fiction "locates itself near the border between factual discourse and fictive discourse, *but does not propose an eradication of that border.* Rather it purports to represent reality by means of agreed-upon conceptions of fictionality, while grafting onto its fictive pact some kind of additional claim to empirical validation" (25; emphasis mine). But this would be to make of testimonio one of the mutations the novel has undergone in the course of its evolution from the Renaissance onward, whereas I want to argue that testimonio involves a break or split with the novel and fictionality as such. There are some other thorny issues embedded here, which I will take up in chapter 5, but for now it may be enough to say that *testimonio is not a form of the novel.*

19. I have overstated here the distinction between testimonio and autobiography, which, as in the distinction between Foley's category of documentary fiction and testimonio noted earlier, is a lot fuzzier in practice. Sylvia Molloy has shown how private autobiography has been a form of collective discourse in Latin American cultural history in *At Face Value* (Cambridge: Cambridge University Press, 1990). There is also what might be called "popular" autobiography, somewhere between literary autobiography and testimonio (for example, *The Autobiography of Malcolm X*, Piri Thomas's *Down These Mean Streets*, or Eduardo Galeano's *Días de amor y guerra*).

Chapter 5. Second Thoughts on Testimonio

1. Gayatri Spivak, "Can the Subaltern Speak?" in *Marxism and the Interpretation of Culture*, ed. C. Nelson and L. Grossberg (Urbana: University of Illinois Press, 1988), p. 278.

2. Rigoberta Menchú, with Elisabeth Burgos-Debray, *I, Rigoberta Menchú: An Indian Woman in Guatemala*, trans. Ann Wright (London: Verso, 1984), p. 1. Wright's translation of this phrase differs from the Spanish, which suggests something more like "the whole truth of a people."

3. Doris Sommer, "Rigoberta's Secrets," *Latin American Perspectives* 70 (1991), p. 48.

4. Alan Cary Webb, "Teaching Third World Auto/Biography: Testimonial Narrative in the Canon and Classroom," *Oregon English* (Fall, 1990), p. 8.

5. See, respectively, Anders Stephanson, "Regarding Postmodernism: A Conversation with Fredric Jameson," *Social Text* 17 (1987); Barbara Harlow, *Resistance Literature* (New York: Methuen, 1987); Barbara Foley, *Telling the Truth: The Theory and Practice of Documentary Fiction* (Ithaca, N.Y.: Cornell University Press, 1986); Margaret Randall, *Testimonios: A Guide to Oral History* (Toronto: Participatory Research Group, 1985); George Yúdice, "Marginality and the Ethics of Survival," in *Universal Abandon? The Politics of Postmodernism*, ed. Andrew

Ross (Minneapolis: University of Minnesota Press, 1988); Gayatri Spivak, "Can the Subaltern Speak?"; and Elzbieta Sklodowska, *Testimonio hispanoamericano* (New York: Peter Lang, 1992). The collections on testimonio include: Hernán Vidal and René Jara eds., *Testimonio y literatura* (Minneapolis: Institute for the Study of Ideologies and Literature, 1986); John Beverley and Hugo Achugar eds., *La voz del otro: Testimonio, Subalternidad y verdad narrativa* (Lima and Pittsburgh: Latinoamérica Editores, 1992); Sherna Gluck and Daphne Patai, *Women's Words: The Feminist Practice of Oral History* (New York: Routledge, 1991); and the special issues of *Latin American Perspectives, Voices of the Voiceless in Testimonial Literature*, 70 (Summer 1991) and 71 (Fall 1991).

6. Roberto González Echevarría, "*Biografía de un cimarrón* and the Novel of the Cuban Revolution," in *The Voice of the Masters: Writing and Authority in Modern Latin American Literature* (Austin: University of Texas Press, 1985).

7. An instance of this ambivalence may be found in the definition of the category of testimonio in the contest rules for the prestigious literary prizes of Cuba's Casa de las Américas: "Testimonios must document some aspect of Latin American or Caribbean reality from a direct source. A direct source is understood as knowledge of the facts by their author and his or her compilation of narratives or evidence obtained from the individuals involved or qualified witnesses. In both cases reliable documentation, written or graphic, is indispensable. The form is at the author's discretion, *but literary quality is also indispensable*" (translation and emphasis mine). But is there a determination of "literary quality" that does not involve in turn an ideology of the literary? Against a modernist bias in favor of textual collage and/ or editorial elaboration in the preparation of a testimonial text, one could argue that a direct, "unliterary" narrative might have both a higher ethical *and* a higher aesthetic status.

8. See, for example, the remarks of the great Peruvian novelist José María Arguedas on the difficulty of reconciling in his own work an inherited Spanish-language model of "literariness" with the representation of the world of Quechua- or Aymara-speaking Andean peasants: "I wrote my first story in the most correct and 'literary' Spanish I could devise. I read the story to some of my writer friends in the capital, and they praised it. But I came to detest more and more those pages. No, what I wanted to describe—one could almost say denounce—wasn't like that at all, not the person, not the town, not the landscape. Under a false language a world appeared as invented, without marrow and without blood: a typically 'literary' world in which the word had consumed the work." "La novela y el problema de la expresión literaria en el Perú," in *Obras completas*, vol. 2 (Lima: Editorial Horizonte, 1983), p. 196; translation mine. Arguedas's solution was to develop a novel in Spanish based stylistically and thematically on the tension between Spanish and Quechua. By contrast, there is the well-known example of the Kenyan writer Ngugi wa

Thiongo who in 1977, after publishing a series of successful anticolonial novels in English, decided to write his novels, plays, and stories exclusively in his tribal language, Kikuyu. See "Language of African Literature," in *Decolonising the Mind: The Politics of Language in African Literature* (Portsmouth, N.H.: Heinemann, 1987).

9. Ana Guadalupe Martínez, *Las cárceles clandestinas de El Salvador* (Mexico City: Casa El Salvador, 1979), pp. 12–14; translation and emphases mine.

10. See Roque Dalton's reconstruction of the life of one of the founders of the Salvadoran Communist party, *Miquel Mármol*, and his own autobiographical novel of the guerrilla underground, *Pobrecito poeta que era yo*. I will come back to the question of Dalton and his relation to testimonio in chapter 6.

11. Walter Mignolo, "Literacy and Colonization: The New World Experience," in *1492–1992: Re/Discovering Colonial Writing (Hispanic Issues* vol. 4), ed. René Jara and Nicholas Spadaccini (Minneapolis: Prisma Institute, 1989), p. 67. Mignolo is careful to distinguish the literacy policies of the colonial and neocolonial state from the contemporary literacy campaigns instituted, for example, by the Cuban and Nicaraguan revolutions and based on the methods of Paolo Freire's "pedagogy of the oppressed," which he sees as a means of empowerment. For an excellent overview of the field today, see David Archer and Patrick Costello, *Literacy and Power: The Latin American Battleground* (London: Earthscan Publications, 1990).

12. Richard Price notes a similar tension in the relation of the runaway slave communities in the interior of Suriname to the Moravian missionaries who taught them reading, writing, and arithmetic: "The toll exacted over the centuries for this privilege remained constant: intense pressure to renounce 'heathen' ways and to break off relations with non-Christian family and kinfolk. Saramakas then as now were caught in this terrible bind, knowing that literacy was a password to an understanding of the outside world and the key to being able to manipulate it, but also knowing that its acquisition entailed what was, for them, a truly Faustian bargain, the willingness to sell their souls." *Alabi's World* (Baltimore and London: Johns Hopkins University Press, 1990), pp. 67–68.

13. By Robert Carr, "Re(-)presentando el testimonio: Notas sobre el cruce divisorio primer mundo/tercer mundo," in *La voz del otro*, pp. 76–81.

14. See, for example, David Stoll, " 'The Land No Longer Gives': Land Reform in Nebaj, Guatemala," *Cultural Survival Quarterly* 14, 4 (1990), pp. 4–9.

15. Sylvia Molloy, "From Serf to Self: The Autobiography of Juan Francisco Manzano," *Modern Language Notes* 104 (1989), p. 417.

16. It is worth noting that these are not mutually exclusive, as the right-wing attackers, claimed; the problem that the Stanford reforms were trying to address is how to read Rigoberta Menchú *with*, not instead of, Shakespeare.

Chapter 6. The Politics of Latin American Postmodernism

1. One of the problems revealed by the electoral defeat of the Sandinistas is that the identification portended in testimonio between a radicalized intelligentsia—represented by the FSLN leadership and upper and middle cadre—and the popular classes had to some extent broken down under the impact of the war with the contras and struggles about policy within the revolutionary bloc itself.

2. George Yúdice, "¿Puede hablarse de postmodernidad en América Latina?" *Revista de crítica literaria latinoamericana* 29 (1989).

3. The bibliography has now become unmanageable. Along with Yúdice's article just mentioned, a good introduction available in translation is Nelly Richard, "Postmodernism and Periphery," *Third Text* 2 (1987–88). Also Neil Larsen, *Modernism and Hegemony*, introduction and chapters 3 and 4 (Minneapolis: University of Minnesota Press, 1990), and his article, discussed in this chapter, "Postmodernism and Imperialism: Theory and Politics in Latin America," *Postmodern Culture* I, 1 (Fall 1990). Jorge Ruffinelli has published two special issues of his journal *Nuevo Texto Crítico* on the topic (nos. 6 and 7, 1990). A collection of essays by the major Latin American theorists of postmodernity, *The Postmodernism Debate in Latin America*, coedited by myself and José Oviedo, is forthcoming as a special issue of *boundary 2* 20, 3 (1993).

4. See Nelson Osorio's interventions in a debate at Dartmouth in *Revista de crítica literaria latinoamericana* 29 (1989), particularly pp. 146–48, and Octavio Paz, "El romanticismo y la poesía contemporánea", *Vuelta* 11, 127 (1987), pp. 26–27.

5. See Baudrillard's *America* and *Cool Memories*. Joan Didion's *Salvador* (1983) is an example of a similar North American production of a dystopian postmodern sublime in relation to Latin America.

6. Neil Larsen, *Modernism and Hegemony*, p. xxxi.

7. Fredric Jameson, *Postmodernism; or, The Cultural Logic of Late Capitalism* (Durham, N.C.: Duke University Press, 1991).

8. Aijaz Ahmad, "Jameson's Rhetoric of Otherness and the 'National Allegory,' " *Social Text* 17 (1987), p. 3.

9. Fredric Jameson, "The Politics of Theory in the Postmodernism Debate," in *The Ideologies of Theory*, vol. 2, *Syntax of History* (Minneapolis: University of Minnesota Press, 1988), p. 111.

10. For the first, see, for example, Antonio Benítez's *La isla que se repite: El Caribe y la pespectiva posmoderna* (Hanover, N.H.: Ediciones del Norte, 1989); for the second, the following remarks by the Argentine philosopher León Rozitchner, in an interview reproduced in *Casa de las Américas* 168 (1988), pp. 165–66, under the title "La posmodernidad es el opio de los pueblos": "So-called postmodern culture is a war that has been won in human subjectivity by the mass media, technology, religion, and the transnational corporations. The domination of everyday life by the military, dissuasion, rule everything. . . . For us to speak of our postmodernism is a cruel joke. What has introduced us

to our postmodernism is the Process; it is a fact of terror and not of culture, as the affluent Europeans enjoy it. There they are postmodernized by wealth; here by terror and poverty" (translation mine).

11. The best representation of the debate is still, in my opinion, *The Anti-Aesthetic: Essays on Postmodern Culture*, ed. Hal Foster (Port Townsend, Wash.: Bay Press, 1983), with its pairing of a version of the Jameson essay with Habermas's "Modernity—An Incomplete Project." See also E. Ann Kaplan, ed., *Postmodernism and Its Discontents* (London: Verso, 1988); Andrew Ross, ed., *Universal Abandon? The Politics of Postmodernism* (Minneapolis: University of Minnesota Press, 1989); and, in Spanish, *Modernidad y postmodernidad*, ed. Josep Picó (Madrid: Alianza Editorial, 1988).

12. I cite here from a manuscript copy. A somewhat modified version of the argument appears in Yúdice's articles "Marginality and the Ethics of Survival" (in *Universal Abandon?*) and "Testimonio and Postmodernism" in the special issue of *Latin American Perspectives* on testimonio, 70 (Summer 1991). For Yúdice's pro-postmodernist views, see his critique of Habermas in "¿Puede hablarse de postmodernidad en América Latina?" (*Revista de crítica literaria latinoamericana* 29 [1989]), and "Postmodernity and Transnational Capitalism in Latin America" in the collection he coedited with Jean Franco and Juan Flores, *On Edge: The Crisis of Contemporary Latin American Culture* (Minneapolis: University of Minnesota Press, 1992).

13. The decisive case was perhaps Foucault's use of Borges in his introduction to *Les Mots et les choses* (Paris: Gallimard, 1966). On the relation of the Latin American Boom and U.S. postmodernist narrative, see Carlos Rincón, "Modernidad periférica y el desafío de lo postmoderno: Perspectivas del arte narrativo latinoamericano," *Revista de crítica literaria latinoamericana* 29 (1989).

14. These forms might include, besides the testimonio and the discursive practices of the Christian base communities Yúdice describes, new kinds of biographical and narrative texts like Tomás Borge's memoirs; *rock nacional; poesía conversacional; nueva trova; poesía de taller*; Alan Bolt's Matagalpa-based theater collective; both avant-garde and primitive painting; *pintas* (graffiti); Nicaraguan women's writing; ecological or "Green" discourse; telenovelas and TV documentary video work by Sandinista and FMLN media collectives.

15. I refer, of course, to Jean-François Lyotard's *The Postmodern Condition* (Minneapolis: University of Minnesota Press, 1984). It should be noted, however, that Lyotard's account collapses together at least three different *ruptures* or "breaks": an epistemological one, having to do with philosophical antifoundationalism, deconstruction, and poststructuralism; an aesthetic one, having to do with with a post-sixties questioning of modernist ideology; and a political one, having to do with the displacement of traditional class or interest-group politics by the new social movements. One might want, therefore, to distinguish postmodernism as an aesthetic ideology (e.g., in the way Christopher Jencks uses the term) from a more generalized postmodern "condi-

tion." My impulse here, however, is not to do this because of the way the aesthetic itself becomes a central category and form of political-social agency in postmodernity.

16. Sandinista ideology and the FSLN, for example, developed in the late fifties as responses to the dominant Browderism of the small Nicaraguan Communist party, which argued, on the model of the wartime Soviet-American alliance, that the working-class movement should subordinate its goals to those of modernizing and pro-American sectors of the bourgeoisie identified precisely with the Somoza regime. On Sandinism and ideological heterogeneity, see Donald Hodges, *The Intellectual Foundations of the Nicaraguan Revolution* (Austin: University of Texas Press, 1986).

17. At a 1988 conference at Casa de las Américas where I had been discussing postmodernism, I was shown by one of the Cuban participants, a literature professor, the press packets the United States Interests Section in Havana sends—unsolicited—to selected Cuban intellectuals and opinion makers. In the area of cultural reportage, the stories dealt almost exclusively with postmodernist painting, music, dance, theater, and so on, as if to suggest that these delights would be theirs if only they embraced the "free world" (and the free market). What the Interests Section perhaps failed to perceive was that this material was much-anticipated and appreciated because a lively *Cuban* production of postmodernist painting, music, dance, theater, and so on, was already taking place "within the revolution" (to recall Fidel's famous dictum). For a glimpse of this, see Gerardo Mosquera and Rachel Weiss, *The Nearest Edge of the World: Art and Cuba Now* (Brookline, Mass.: Polarities, 1990).

18. I cite here from the manuscript copy presented at the 1990 MLA session on Postmodernism in Latin America. The essay has since appeared in the on-line journal *Postmodern Culture* I, 1 (Fall 1990), accessible on internet from pmc@ncsuvm.ncsu.edu. A Spanish version appeared in *Nuevo Texto Crítico* 6 (1990).

19. Larsen quotes Cornel West's observation that "Americans are politically always already in a condition of postmodern fragmentation and heterogeneity in a way that Europeans have not been; and the revolt against the center by those constituted as marginals is an *oppositional* difference in a way that poststructuralist notions of difference are not." West's reference is to *North* Americans, but the point could be extended to cover Americans (and Canadians?) generally. "Interview with Cornel West," in *Universal Abandon?*, p. 273.

20. Larsen uses the translation of *Miguel Mármol* by Kathleen Ross and Richard Schaff (Willimantic, Conn.: Curbstone, 1982).

21. Ernesto Laclau, "Towards a Theory of Populism," in his *Politics and Ideology in Marxist Theory* (London: New Left Books, 1977). Larsen has a more extensive discussion of Laclau and "culturalism" in the introduction to *Modernism and Hegemony*, pp. xxvi–xxi.

22. "The interaction of the historiographic and the metafictional foregrounds the rejection of the claims of both 'authentic' representation

and 'inauthentic' copy alike, and the very meaning of artistic originality is as forcefully challenged as is the transparency of historical
referentiality. Postmodern fiction suggests that to re-write or to represent the past in fiction and history is, in both cases, to open it up
to the present, to prevent it from being conclusive and teleological."
Linda Hutcheon, *A Poetics of Postmodernism* (New York: Routledge,
1988), p. 110.

23. There is now something like a "new wave" in Latin American media
criticism influenced by postmodernism: see, for example, Néstor
García Canclini, *Culturas híbridas: Estrategias para entrar y salir de la
modernidad* (Mexico City: Grijalbo, 1990).

24. Perhaps the most influential articulation of the relation between modernism and the revolutionary left was Che Guevara's remarks on art
and literature in his essay *On Man and Socialism in Cuba*.

25. Stanley Aronowitz, "Postmodernism and Politics," in *Universal Aban-
don?*, pp. 60–61. The major theoretical manifesto of the "radical dem-
ocratic" politics of new social movements has been, of course, Ernesto
Laclau and Chantal Mouffe, *Hegemony and Socialist Strategy* (London:
Verso, 1985). See also *The Making of Social Movements in Latin America:
Identity, Strategy, and Democracy*, ed. Arturo Escobar and Sonia Alvarez
(Boulder, Colo.: Westview Press, 1992).

26. Jameson, in a recent revision of his own concept of postmodernism,
has noted in this respect that: "the postmodern may well in that sense
be little more than a transitional period between two stages of capitalism, in which the earlier forms of the economic are in the process
of being restructured on a global scale, including the older forms of
labor and its traditional organizational institutions and concepts. That
a new international proletariat (taking forms we cannot yet imagine)
will reemerge from this convulsive upheaval it needs no prophet to
predict: we ourselves are still in the trough, however, and no one can
say how long we will stay there" (*Postmoderism* 417).

27. Adolfo Sánchez Vázquez, "Posmodernidad, posmodernismo y soci-
alismo," *Casa de las Américas* 175 (1989), p. 145 (translation mine).

Chapter 7. The Ideology of Postmodern Music and Left Politics

1. Theodor Adorno, "Perennial Fashion—Jazz," in *Prisms*, trans. Sam-
uel Weber and Shierry Weber (London: Neville Spearman, 1967), pp.
128–29. See also his "On Popular Music," *Studies in Philosophy and the
Social Sciences* 9 (1941).

2. See Adorno, *The Philosophy of Modern Music*, trans. Anne Mitchell and
Wesley Blomster (New York: Seabury Press, 1980), pp. 129–33.

3. Christa Bürger, "The Disappearance of Art: The Postmodernism Debate in the U.S.," *Telos* 68 (Summer 1986), pp. 93–106. She is echoed
in this by Jameson in part II, Parable of the Oarsmen, of *Late Marxism:
Adorno, or the Persistence of the Dialectic* (London: Verso, 1990).

4. Ilhan Mimaroglu, extracts from an interview with John Cage in record
album notes for Berio, Cage, Mimaroglu, *Electronic Music* (Turnabout
TV34046S).

5. Jean-Paul Sartre, *Nausea*, trans. Lloyd Alexander (New York: New Directions, 1959), pp. 33–36.

6. Cf. the following remarks by the minimalist composer La Monte Young: "Around 1960 I became interested in yoga, in which the emphasis is on concentration and focus on the sounds inside your head. Zen meditation allows ideas to come and go as they will, which corresponds to Cage's music; he and I are like opposites which help define each other. . . . In singing, when the tone becomes perfectly in tune with a drone, it takes so much concentration to keep it in tune that it drives out all other thoughts. You become one with the drone and one with the Creator." Cited in Kyle Gann, "La Monte Young: Maximal Spirit," *Village Voice*, June 9, 1987, p. 70.

7. "Beethoven's symphonies in their most arcane chemistry are part of the bourgeois process of production and express the perennial disaster brought on by capitalism. But they also take a stance of tragic affirmation towards reality as a social fact; they seem to say that the status quo is the best of all possible worlds. Beethoven's music is as much a part of the revolutionary emancipation of the bourgeoisie as it anticipates the latter's apologia. The more profoundly you decode works of art, the less absolute is their contrast to praxis." Theodor Adorno, *Aesthetic Theory*, trans. C. Lenhardt (New York: Routledge, 1986), p. 342.

8. Eugene Genovese, *Roll, Jordan, Roll: The World the Slaves Made* (New York: Vintage, 1976), pp. 159–280.

9. Pierre Lere, *"Free Jazz*: Evolution ou Révolution," *Revue d'Esthétique* 3–4, 1970, cited in Herbert Marcuse, *Counterrevolution and Revolt* (Boston: Beacon Press, 1972), p. 114.

10. Jacques Attali, *Noise: The Political Economy of Music*, trans. Brian Massumi (Minneapolis: University of Minnesota Press, 1985).

11. That is why I argued at the beginning of chapter 1 against the notion of booklike "textuality" deployed by deconstruction. Barthes is one exception, but there are others; for something like a primer of poststructuralist music theory, John Mowitt suggests I. Stoianova, *Geste, Texte, Musique* (Paris: 10/18, 1985).

12. The semiotic for Kristeva is a sort of babble out of which language arises—something between glossolalia and the pre-oedipal awareness of the sounds of the mother's body. As such, its reemergence undermines the subject's submission to the Symbolic, that is, the dimension of law and culture, "fixed" identity. "Kristeva makes the case that the semiotic is the effect of bodily drives which are incompletely repressed when the paternal order has intervened in the mother/child dyad, and it is therefore 'attached' psychically to the mother's body." Paul Smith, *Discerning the Subject* (Minneapolis: University of Minnesota Press, 1988), p. 121.

13. Fredric Jameson, *The Political Unconscious: Narrative as a Socially Symbolic Act* (Ithaca, N.Y.: Cornell University Press, 1981), pp. 288–91.

14. Jameson notes the paradox that Adorno himself may be counted

among the progenitors of a theory of postmodernist music in his concept of "informal music" in the essay "Vers une musique informelle"):
Late Marxism, pp. 246–47.

15. Russell Berman, "Modern Art and Desublimation," *Telos* 62 (Winter
1984–85), p. 48.

16. Given the relation between modernization and rationalization, it has
seemed paradoxically necessary for capitalist merchandising to pre-
serve or inject some semblance of precapitalist aura in the commodity—hence kitsch (Disneyland, the Golden Arches)—whereas socialized production should in principle have no problem with loss of
aura, since it is not implicated in the commodity status of a use-value
or good. Postmodernist pastiche or *mode rétro*—where a signifier of
aura is alluded to or incorporated, but in an ironic and playful way—
seems an intermediate position, in the sense that it can function both
to endow the commodity with an "arty" quality or to detach aspects
of commodity aesthetics from commodity production and circulation
per se, as in Warhol.

17. John Cage, *Silence* (Cambridge, Mass.: MIT Press, 1966), p. 76.

18. "Yet this sense of freedom and possibility—which is for the course of
the 60s a momentarily objective reality, as well as (from the hindsight
of the 80s) a historical illusion—may perhaps best be explained in
terms of the superstructural movement and play enabled by the transition from one infrastructural or systemic stage of capitalism to another." Fredric Jameson, "Periodizing the 60s," in *The 60s Without
Apology*, ed. Sohnya Sayres et al. (Minneapolis: *Social Text*/University
of Minnesota Press, 1984), p. 208.

19. In Isabelle Anscombe and Dike Blair, eds., *Punk!* (New York: Urizen,
1978).

20. Simon Frith, *Sound Effects: Youth, Leisure and the Politics of Rock 'n' Roll*
(New York: Pantheon, 1981), pp. 264–68.

21. *Ibid.*, p. 268. Cf. Andreas Huyssen: "The growing sense that we are
not bound to *complete* the project of modernity (Habermas' phrase)
and still do not necessarily have to lapse into irrationality or into
apocalyptic frenzy, the sense that art is not exclusively pursuing some
telos of abstraction, non-representation, and sublimity—all of this has
opened up a host of possibilities for creative endeavors today." *After
the Great Divide: Modernism, Mass Culture, Postmodernism* (Blooming-
ton: Indiana University Press, 1986), p. 217.

22. Huyssen notes perceptively that "given the aesthetic field-force of the
term postmodernism, no neo-conservative today would dream of
identifying the neo-conservative project as postmodern" (*After the
Great Divide*, 204).

23. Jesse Lemisch, "I Dreamed I Saw MTV Last Night," *The Nation* (October 18, 1986), pp. 361, 374–76; and Lemisch's reply to the debate that
ensued, "The Politics of Left Culture," *The Nation* (December 20,
1986), pp. 700ff.

Index

John Beverley, professor of Hispanic languages and literatures at the University of Pittsburgh, has published extensively on the problems of narrative, history, ideology, subalternity, politics, imperialism, and revolution. His *Literature and Politics in the Central American Revolutions* (1990—coauthored with Marc Zimmerman) has been widely reviewed in academic and popular media.